Hurricane

Robert Bahr

Dedicated to

Robert Henry

CONTENTS

July, 1989

MONDAY

CHAPTER I

At the helm of a rusting red and white tug named for his ex-wife, Barbara, Doyle Donahue surveyed the island. For more than a decade, he'd plied this route from the coal terminals of New Orleans to the power generating plants north of Pensacola. Along that route, no sight was as dreamy and lonely as the white sand, green foliage, and blue sky of Dauphin Island's west end. When he gazed upon it, the hard lines of his face, weathered well beyond his 32 years, softened.

He reached for the half empty Jim Beam bottle, perched like a mascot on the tug's console of knobs, dials, and switches. Doyle took a long swig and wiped his mouth on his sleeve. He looked out over the hopper barge his *Barbara* pushed, 35 feet wide, 195 feet long, so long he could hardly see Al Reed at the bow waving his one good arm. Al kept the tug and barge between the red and green flashing buoys of the channel, hidden from Doyle by the massive load of coal. He'd wave his good arm or the hook furiously to port or starboard. Two thousand tons of coal and steel between Doyle and his mate glided smoothly along the narrow channel, the sun reflecting from ten thousand gleaming facets as though they were black diamonds.

He'd awakened this morning with his face in a pool of spilled whiskey on the galley table, shrill pain piercing the back of his skull. He'd grown used to hangovers, but never had he felt like this, a blade stabbing into his brain with every heartbeat. To dull the agony, he'd had a beer, and another as he and Al had made up the barge in New Orleans.

It was a tedious but critical process, dropping the loop of wire cable over the steel bits on each side of the barge, running them around cleats port and starboard on the tug, then to the manual winches at the bow. He tightened them as best he could with a hand crank, no match for the electric winches on the newer tugs. Cabled up that way on both sides with inch-thick wire and a two-inch soft line of hemp from the tug to the barge, the two would move through the water like a single unit. Of course there was always some play, and Doyle realized as he looked out from the pilothouse to the tug's deck there was more slack today than usual. Whenever a strong breeze blew from the southwest, the starboard cable grew taut and the port loosened noticeably. He would tighten them again when he and Al reached Mobile Bay, just beyond the bridge.

The bridge was still a mile ahead, light traffic moving in both directions. He could see the traffic above the coal through the haze of humidity. The span stretched from Cedar Point on the Alabama mainland across three miles of shallows and sand spits to Dauphin Island, fifteen to twenty feet above the water, except where the bridge crossed the channel. There it rose almost 50 feet above the water.

The tug approached the heart of Dauphin Island: the tall pines and original settlement, the old village where Doyle himself lived. Along the shore, the docks where commercial shrimpers tied their 50-foot rigs and Doyle kept his tug lay empty now. Next to the slips, Lou Parrish's Pelican Pub hung out over the water, its glass walls facing east, north, and west along the Sound. Across the street from the cafe, Randy Manning's garage stood high and commanding, a gray cinder block barn surrounded by rusting cars, trucks, boats, engines, hoods, fenders, and a front-end loader.

By now, Doyle could see the bridge clearly rising above the mountain of coal. He shook his head to clear his thinking. The pounding engine, clanging channel markers, and shrill squeal of the VHF radio suddenly seemed to explode in his head. He rested his forehead in the palm of his hand, moaning.

Finally, locking the wheel in place, he went below to find aspirin. The bottle was just where it belonged, in the medicine kit behind the mirror in the head.

A loud metallic twang screamed over the tug's pounding engine. Instantly the vessel lurched sharply to starboard. Doyle raced up the ladder to the pilothouse. He saw Al Reed climbing to his feet on a heap of coal and waving furiously. The starboard cable had snapped, slashing the air like a giant whip. Now it dragged beneath the tug.

Slowly, with the port cable still restraining the barge, it turned perpendicular to the bridge. Doyle calmly slowed the engine, threw the tug into reverse, opened the throttle. The barge was no more than one hundred yards from the bridge now, the length of a football field, but slowly, slowly the massive form began to lose speed.

We're gonna make it, Doyle thought.

It seemed their forward movement had ceased.

The jolt as the tug's huge propeller ground into mud hurled Doyle backward. He saw the port cable whip violently above the barge, thrash the air, and come to rest on the coal.

4

Doyle gazed at the traffic flowing on the bridge.

Getting to his feet, Al, too, turned to the bridge. In the silence of the steamy afternoon, the barge drifted with the current, a leviathan in patient pursuit of its prey.

Turning to Doyle, Al threw his arm and hook wide in silent pleading. Doyle stared at him blankly. Finally, Al gazed at the water and jumped.

Doyle raced to the bow. "Go back! Go back!" he screamed, waving his arms wildly, knowing they wouldn't understand, probably wouldn't even see him.

"Go back, back," he whispered, and dropped his hands.

In disbelief Doyle watched the barge ram the barnacle-encrusted wooden fenders protecting the concrete support columns. The timbers cracked and shattered.

The roar of the collision tumbled across the water. The barge had rammed the pilings dead center with an inertial force of almost four million pounds. The reinforced concrete support shattered top to bottom, great chunks of it crashing down onto the coal where Al Reed had stood.

The steel rods supporting the roadbed bent. Huge sections of concrete broke loose and crashed into the sound. A white convertible plunged into the abyss, voices screaming, then overwhelmed by the roar of the collapsing bridge section.

Doyle heard the shriek of rubber on asphalt, saw a blue Oldsmobile slip over the jagged edge of concrete and metal and drop twenty feet into the rubble.

On the island side of the bridge, a red BMW convertible had almost cleared the destroyed span, and now dangled in space, its rear axle and wheels missing. Only the weight of its engine on the island's asphalt kept it from plunging into the Sound.

CHAPTER II

"Throw me a ring, will you for God's sake?" Al Reed yelled from the shallows, where he was chest-deep in water and mud. Slowly Doyle turned to him, his face ashen. He reached for the life ring and threw it. Al clung to it with his good hand as, mechanically, Doyle pulled him through the murky water to the tug. He lifted his mate into the vessel, and rushed back into the damaged pilothouse, picked up the VHF radio and dialed a number from memory.

"I gotta get in touch with Randy Manning," he told Al. "He'll know what to do!"

———

Norman Whitney jogged nude along the windward shore on the far west end of Dauphin Island, the Gulf of Mexico to his left. He moved like a lightly tanned cheetah, with long, graceful strides, splashing through the foam and blue-green waves. The well-formed body seemed a natural part of the island, like the sea gulls drifting on warm air currents a few feet above him. His wide lips, framed by a neatly trimmed beard and mustache, suggested a perpetual smile.

Here, alone, one with the sand, sea, and sky, he felt himself in harmony with the universe. Sandpipers chased receding waves, picking at morsels of flesh left behind. Ghost crabs, their antenna-like eyes bulging, skittered near the water's edge.

Along the high tide line, a ribbon of debris stretched to the horizon—broken shells, plastic cups, drying slime of jellyfish tentacles. Above the line, white sand flowed in unbroken monotony to the east and west. Inland, where Norman sometimes ran, the sand rose in dunes adorned with pink-blossomed railroad vines, delicate white beach morning glories, rosemary bushes, and goldenrods.

Farther inland, motionless in the shade of scrub oaks and palmettos, raccoons hid from the heat. A bull alligator moaned from an impenetrable thicket of saw grass, slash pine, yucca, and a few toothache trees.

He approached a point where the island flattened. Here, countless storms had swept Gulf waves across the sand into the Mississippi Sound, narrowing the island's width to a few hundred feet. He saw the muddy water of the sound rippling lazily along the pristine shoreline. It lapped at the scrub grass and sun-bleached logs, parched oyster shells and fish bones.

Nothing in the heat and haze seemed to move except the nibbling wavelets along the sand. But along that leeward stretch of scrub, he heard the soft hum and saw the black mist-like swarms of gnats, expanding and contracting in primordial rhythm as they searched for blood. A great blue heron stood motionless on one leg, tiny black eyes riveted on the shallows in search of shrimp. Suddenly she struck, retrieved a young mullet, startling a nearby stingray into fleeing to deeper water.

———

Far in the distance, Norman heard what he assumed to be rolling thunder.

CHAPTER III

Lying on a sunlit bed in the master bedroom of her Gulf-side home, Abby Marwick ran her fingers through Randy Manning's rusty blond hair. She caressed him teasingly around his ears, locked her fingers behind his neck and pulled his face into her breasts. He moaned in pleasure.

She caressed his back and buttocks with feather-like strokes. He stretched, accepting her touch with a boyish grin.

The first time Abby Marwick had stepped into Manning's Garage a month earlier, the huge cluttered space reminded her of a boy's playroom—tools, tires, batteries, car parts scattered haphazardly over the sprawling floor. A blue Pontiac squatted in the center of the chaos, its hood removed, its motor lying next to it on the concrete. A transmission lay beside a red Comanche.

Randy was at the far end of the garage sanding the hull of a boat when he heard the car door slam. Wiping the sweat from his forehead, he stood tall and lanky, blond hair disheveled, two days' growth of stubble on his face.

Abby wore a simple but expensive tennis outfit, white with aquamarine trim. Randy's eyes went first to her long, shapely legs. He noted the shoulder-length black hair. It cascaded over her breasts, the ends bobbing with each movement of her shoulders.

She was young—Randy guessed in her mid-20s.

"Can I help you ma'am?" The leathery skin of his face tightened in a smile.

"My ca's overheating," she scolded. "I have no idea why."

"Me neither," Randy said with a shrug, still smiling. "I'd be happy to check it if you want, ma'am."

His charm seemed too endearing, too innocent to be spontaneous. Yet, she warmed to him.

"That's why I'm here," she said.

"Sure." He started for the car.

"I guess you're Randy Manning," she said.

"Yep. Have been all my life." He reached into the car and pulled the hood release. Abby noticed the strong, sinewy arms.

"Everyone knows you, it seems."

"Everybody knows everybody that's here year-round. It's only a few hundred. Of course I'm the only garage. It's me or the mainland."

"That's what they said."

He lifted the hood. "You're right—your motor's running hot," he said. "Probably losing water."

"What would cause that, Randy Manning? This is no piece of junk, you know."

"I know that, ma'am. This here's a Porscher, one of the finest machines made in the whole world. But, you know, water pumps go out on Porschers same as on Chevys and Fords. Or maybe a hose sprung a leak, or one of them big tires on an eighteen-wheeler shot a stone right through your radiator. It could be a million things, ma'am."

"Why not call me Abby, Randy Manning?"

Smiling broadly, he extended a large, calloused hand, retracted it to wipe against his jeans, and reached out again. She took his fingers, laughing.

"Abby Marwick." She held his fingers for a moment, teasing him with her eyes. "Can you fix it or not?"

"I can fix anything."

"When?"

"Well, that's the problem, Abby. I got work coming out my ears. And I'm trying to get the *Island Maiden* in shape for some fishing. That there boat over there—it's the fastest thing on the water here to Biloxi."

"To hell with your boat," she said, her eyes suddenly fiery. "I want that car fixed by tomorrow. I'll pay whatever it takes."

"Tell you what," Randy said lightly, "I'll do everything I can for you." His large blue eyes held her steadily, his voice deep, raspy. "I mean, I want to make my customers happy, you know. But I can't be rushed if I'm gonna do the job right."

Although they were several feet apart, Abby smelled the odor of him.

"You take your time?" She spoke softly, moving closer.

"That's what a professional does, Abby. Quality work takes time."

He'd driven her home that afternoon, to the new, circular, reinforced concrete structure facing the Gulf. All winter the permanent residents had whispered in speculation about its peculiar size and shape.

"It'll hold up against any hurricane," she told Randy while they climbed the stairs to the deck. "The joists are tied into the frame, and the roof's bolted to the joists. Steel shutters protect all the glass, and the whole thing's held down by tons of concrete under the sand."

"Sounds like a fort," Randy commented.

11

He undressed her on the lush white great room carpet, the blue-green waves of the Gulf dancing to the shore and dissolving into lacy foam not 30 feet away. He played with her, smiling as she breathed rapidly. He ran his callused palm across her cheek, down her neck, her shoulder, her breast.

"We got time, Abby—ma'am." She sensed sarcasm in the way he said that word. "I'm gonna tease you till you can't stand it no more."

For more than an hour he used his hands, mouth and body to overwhelm her with wave on wave of pleasure, her hair matting to her damp skin, her body draining of energy until she was utterly without strength.

"You got a nice place here, Abby," he commented, walking through the dining room and kitchen to the library at the back, where he could gaze across Bienville Boulevard to the remains of a storm-wrecked house, the private fishing pier next to it reaching into the dark water of the sound.

He returned to find Abby asleep on the carpet, her arms outstretched, her breasts rising and falling rhythmically. He studied the contours of her body at length, enjoying her as he would a work of art. After a time, he turned back through the library and left by the rear door.

It's not like I don't love Cookie, he thought, as he drove back to the garage. Sex was just a game—his favorite game, actually, and had nothing to do with love. She did whatever he asked sexually, even some things he didn't ask for, loved him, doted on him. And he loved her, more deeply than he could explain. He knew that. But she'd grown familiar. The lust faded, and lust was one of the few things that made him feel truly alive.

It was like facing a real challenge, even danger. Those two things—lust and danger—did something crazy to his head. He heard *music*, like violins in a moonlit, cloudless night. In those rare moments, his heart pumping adrenalin, he felt apart from the noise and confusion around him; his mind grew sharp as a razor. He transcended everything, became ecstatic.

He began seeing Abby Marwick almost daily. The Porsche remained parked in the garage behind the *Island Maiden*, the new water pump in its unopened container stored on the car's roof. Abby drove the old Chevy Lumina Randy lent her.

Again that Monday, unaware the bridge was out, he touched her and set Abby to shivering. His hands moved along her thighs with the firmness and confidence of his mastery. Yet, it was a controlled and gentle touch, insisting on her surrender, caressing her in gratitude. He studied her body, his gaze enforcing the words he whispered: "You're beautiful."

She stretched and arched up to him, dropping her head back to expose her neck to his lips. She whimpered softly, began a low moan that finally climaxed in uncontrollable spasms. A moment later, he collapsed on her, his face between her breasts. She kissed his hair.

"You're a wonderful boy, Randy Manning," she whispered, caressing his neck. "I like you very much."

———

At the garage, Don Long wiped greasy hands on his overalls and answered the phone.

"Randy's not here," he told Doyle. Oh, shit, that's terrible! Yeah, I think I know where he is. I'll page him." He hung up and dialed Randy Manning's pager. A moment later the telephone in the garage rang.

"Sure it's an emergency!" Don yelled over the screaming firehouse siren a block away. "Everything's *always* an emergency. Got a fire, call Manning, volunteer fire chief. Major catastrophe? Manning's Civil Defense. Somebody disturbing the peace? Ain't no such thing as a police department on Dauphin Island. Call Manning. He'll muscle a citizen's arrest, hold the guy till the sheriff's department gets here from the mainland in a day or two. I'm telling you, Randy, I can't keep filling in all the gaps for you. It's driving me nuts."

"The emergency, Don," Randy said softly, "what's the emergency?"

Don paused for breath, clearing his throat. "The bridge is out. People are hurt. First I phoned the dispatcher at the firehouse so she could signal the volunteers. Then I called you. Now what should I do?"

"Get the *Island Maiden* in the water. I'll be there right away."

———

Don Long slammed the telephone receiver down and sprinted to the door. "Damn," he said to himself, shaking his head. He jogged to his truck, backed it to the trailer supporting Randy's boat, and within minutes, had the *Island Maiden* launched and tied at the dock.

He ran to the bridge half a block away. Breathless, he slowed to a walk. The scene reminded him of a World War II movie—fifty feet of bridge gone, a twisted steel I-beam jutting up out of the sound like the remains of a bombed-out building.

Slabs of bridge had fallen on and around the barge. The fragments of wooden fenders had drifted on the current well into Mobile Bay. Several oystermen had already set off in their small white wooden boats after the most dangerous debris, and were towing it out of the shipping lanes. They steered clear of the submerged concrete and I-beams of the bridge itself.

Don approached the precipice. To his left he saw a young woman with long black hair stepping over the windshield of a red BMW convertible and sliding across the hood to the pavement. Beside him on the right, the motor of a black Cadillac limousine hummed smoothly. Don turned to the driver. She was a woman in her late fifties, her hair dyed red, her face square and leathery. She returned his gaze with a dry, humorless expression.

"You almost bought the farm," he shouted over the wailing siren.

She pushed a button, lowering the window. "No kidding? I'm a goddamn inch from being dead."

"It's a real mess."

"*You're* telling *me*? I'm out of Scotch, and the liquor store's on *that* side of the bridge."

Randy Manning drove up in his rickety truck and leaped out. He ran to Don's side.

"Jesus," he muttered, "it's unbelievable. Is the *Maiden* ready?"

"Just like you wanted. Fueled and ready to go."

Randy turned and sprinted toward the docks.

"What's your name, lady?" Don yelled to the woman in the Caddy. She opened the door and stepped out.

"Ruth—Ruth Knebles." With an expression more like a scowl than the concern it reflected, she gazed repeatedly from Don to the cars below.

The siren on the roof of the firehouse grew silent.

Ruth and Don watched as Randy slowly nudged the *Island Maiden* closer to the heap of debris and two cars. He helped a man from one of them and carried him to the boat. From the other care he led three girls. All seemed uninjured.

"We were wearing safety belts!" one exclaimed.

"We landed on the wheels!" another announced.

"That was a hell of a hard landing," the third declared.

"Now, that's a miracle," Ruth mumbled. "By all rights, they should be dead."

"Yes, ma'am," Don said, nodding vigorously. "They'real lucky."

Ruth studied Don, her lips pursed, her head to one side. Finally she said, "I guess you'll do."

"Do what?"

"Drive me home. I'm too nervous to drive."

"Sure, Ruth. Any time."

As Don slipped behind the Cadillac's steering wheel, Ruth Knebles confronted the crowd in a shrill voice: "Get out of the way! I can't sit here all day. I'm not getting any younger. We're turning this boat around. I'm talking to *you*, buster—throw your ass in reverse!" With the flick of both wrists, she drove the crowd back. A moment later they were moving along LeMoyne Avenue to Bienville Boulevard.

"It's Seaview Condos," she told Don. "Left here, right at Hernando. I'm the last apartment on the right."

"Yes, ma'am."

He pulled to the curb. The Gulf of Mexico sparkled in the late afternoon sun.

Ruth reached over and squeezed Don's forearm. "Reminds me of my Frederico when he was a young man—rippled stomach, gorgeous ass, the sexiest man, and so considerate. I hate his guts, the son of a bitch."

Don laughed. "You must be talking about your husband," he guessed.

"Who else?" Ruth said. "My ex-husband-to-be. The quicker the better."

"I'm sorry."

"What for?"

Don shot her a quick glance. She saw the pity in his eyes. "It was a rotten thing to do, throwing you over at this time of your life," he said.

"Hah! Just what I'd expect from a man. I'm the one dumping him. I never complained about the numbers or even the bootlegging, but I told him no hard drugs—no *drugs!* I won't have young kids getting into that shit. But it's all power with him, the two-bit Mussolini. Well, he's gonna pay, that's for sure."

For a while they were silent. Finally, Ruth said, "You wouldn't know of a man looking for a job, would you?"

"Doing what, ma'am?"

"I need a bodyguard."

Ruth saw the apprehension in his face. "Well, a kind of chauffeur, handyman, companion—that sort of thing."

Don sighed. He smiled. "Well, that'd sure be a nice job for some lucky man," he said. "Of course, I work at Manning's Garage."

"I know. I've seen you there. You don't seem happy."

"I'm not." He shook his head. "Randy's the greatest guy in the world, but he just ain't no businessman. Everywhere you look, there's unfinished jobs. We got an air conditioner—who knows what's wrong with it—a tire needs a patch, parts from a truck body, that damned Porsche, at least six cars waiting to get fixed. The phone rings off the hook all day, old ladies screaming at me, like it's my fault Randy can't stick to one job long enough to get anything done."

Don sighed. "But it's a job," he said. "Three hundred and fifty a week—when he pays me."

"I'll start you at four-fifty, room and board, and bonuses now and then."

"Well, now," Don's eyes widened. He grinned broadly. "That's a lot of money just for driving you around." With a sly glance, he waved his finger at her. "I see what you're getting at," he said.

"No you don't, you dimwit. But you will soon enough."

"Well, all right," Don said, still grinning and fluttering his eyelashes. He pulled up to the curb in front of the last apartment on Condo Lane. Fifty feet ahead, waves rolled gently over the sand.

Walking around the car, Don opened the passenger door and Ruth stepped out.

"Thank you," she said curtly, ignoring his gleeful smile.

"You're welcome, Ruth."

CHAPTER IV

Leaving Doyle Donahue to tie the tug at its slip near the Pelican Pub, Al Reed dashed across the road to Manning's Garage. By then, Don Long had already spoken to Randy and had gone to the bridge. When Al found no one at the garage, he panicked. Racing into the yard, he searched between rows of junk yelling, "Randy! Randy, where the hell are you, for the love of God?" Finally, he stopped and crumbled onto an old truck tire.

"It's just no use," he gasped.

At that moment, Randy ran into the yard searching for life vests and a coil of rope. Al leaped to his feet. The small, balding man gestured wildly with his good arm.

"All hell's broke loose, Randy," he shouted. "Some damn fool rammed the bridge with a barge!" He stared at the ground. "It's a real mess, cars in the water. God, it's scary."

"I know. I been there. I'm on my way back soon's I can get some equipment." He stopped speaking and walked toward Al. "Say, how do you know what it's like? I thought you were running out of New Orleans with Doyle this week."

His eyes widening, Randy demanded, "Where's Doyle?"

"Aw, hell," Al mumbled, still staring at the ground. "It's the terriblest thing, Randy. I don't know how he did it. I was up there on the barge— damn near got killed. I ain't even seen him since we got to the slip. Guess he's gone to his place."

Randy shook his head. "I gotta go. If anybody wants me, tell 'em I'm at the bridge in my boat."

He jogged to the garage office for the life vests and rope. There he found a middle-aged man in a white dress shirt, brown slacks and expensive loafers sitting in the office, somber, his arms folded across his chest.

"Are you Randy?" he asked.

"Yeah. Look, I got a hell of a situation here."

"I know. I heard about it—several times. I'm Norman Whitney. My car's stuck in the sand out on the west end."

"Get in touch with me tomorrow. There's these girls in the water."

"Of course. Look, I'll go with you. Perhaps you can use a hand."

"In a white shirt, slacks, and fancy shoes?"

"You might need help."

"Well then, let's go!" The two men sprinted across the street to where Don had tied the *Island Maiden.*

———

Al Reed shuffled off to the far corner of the garage, found the push broom, hooked the handle under the armpit of his good hand and gripped it firmly. "Let them be heroes if they want," he grumbled to Blackie, the Labrador who lay on the cool concrete in a shady corner. "It ain't what it's cracked up to be. Now git, you dumb dog—can't you see I'm sweeping?"

———

One-thirty that afternoon, with Norman sitting in the bow, Randy nudged his fifteen-foot outboard gently toward the barge. Overhead, helicopters from two Mobile television stations hovered, their downdrafts complicating Randy's control of the boat. Glancing north to the mainland, he saw the red and blue flashing lights of state police cars. No doubt the sheriff's department would be on hand, too. He picked up the VHF microphone, turned the dial to channel sixteen, and shouted over the noise of the helicopters, "This is Randy Manning calling Dauphin Island Dispatch. Lucy, do you read?"

"I hear you loud and clear, Randy. Where've you been?"

"I'm on the water at the bridge. Switch to channel thirty-two." He turned the dial quickly. "Lucy, do you read?"

"Loud and clear."

"Okay. Get some volunteers to clear the cars and sightseers from what's left of the bridge on our side. Put up roadblocks. Anybody called the Coast Guard?"

"I did. I didn't have much to tell them."

"Never mind, I see their buoy tender coming from the bay now. I'll get them on the radio. How about calling Southern Salvage. We're gonna need a barge with the biggest crane they've got. Over and out."

Randy turned the dial back to the emergency channel. "This is Randy Manning calling the Coast Guard buoy tender *Bay Way* east of the bridge. Come in, Coast Guard. Over."

"This is the Coast Guard tender *Bay Way*. Over."

"The channel's closed off—a forty foot chunk of bridge is out. Some of it's in the water, some on a coal barge. Over."

"How'd it happen?"

"Runaway barge. That's all I know. Right now, we need to close the sound to shipping. I'll get a couple salvage crews working on this mess, see if we can't open the channel before too long—we'll have barges backed up here to New Orleans. First I gotta get some young ladies out of the water and on dry land. Over and out."

In fact, no one had died at the bridge. The driver of the white convertible had swerved so violently the car shot clear of the barge and bridge debris and plummeted into the channel, all four wheels striking the water simultaneously. The four teenaged girls popped to the surface like corks. Within a few strokes, they were out of the channel and standing in three feet of water on a sand bar surrounded by deep water. Now they screamed for help and waved their arms.

Hanging up the microphone, Randy moved the boat slowly forward. With Norman warning him of submerged objects, Randy weaved the *Maiden* around debris and approached the girls.

————

Jessica Lofton spoke to one of the men in yellow hardhats who were directing traffic and setting up roadblocks.

"That's my car right there," she explained. "The red one."

He whistled. "With luck like that, you oughtta buy some lottery tickets. We'll tow it to Manning's soon as we can."

"Will you get my suitcase? It's in the front. I just don't want to go near the edge." She shuddered. "I'm still terrified."

"No problem, ma'am." He dashed to the car and returned with a red suitcase.

"Thank you," Jessica said, smiling.

"No problem, ma'am."

The temperature was 96 by then, the air steamy. Clutching her suitcase, Jessica started along the treeless asphalt road toward Bienville Boulevard and the Bluebird Motel.

After a quarter of a mile, her long black hair grew matted with sweat. The damp white blouse plastered itself to her body.

The suitcase grew heavier, almost too heavy to carry, it seemed. She paused, switched hands, and pressed on.

When she reached the water tower, she stopped under the dense shade of a water oak. Sitting on her red suitcase and leaning back against the tree, she closed her eyes and breathed deeply.

Finally she regained her strength and stood, dusted off the suitcase, and started west toward the Bluebird Motel sign.

She stumbled through the office door and collapsed on a yellow vinyl sofa.

A large black woman in her mid-thirties scrambled to her feet from behind the counter, where she'd been watching an afternoon soap.

"Oh, my, you look awful!" she declared.

Jessica offered a wan smile. "I'm not feeling great," she said, her voice raspy. "I shouldn't be walking, especially in this heat. My car's on the bridge—most of it, anyway."

"Dear God, honey, was you on that bridge?"

"I was…the last one to get across it, in fact. Well almost. My rear end's gone."

The woman's eyes widened in astonishment. "Honey, how you be walkin' with no rear end?"

Jessica smiled, then laughed. "My *car's* rear axle just dropped right off," she corrected.

"Well, here, now," the woman said, bustling to Jessica's side, "Let's get you some coffee."

"Thank you. Later, perhaps. Right now I need a room with a good shower, air conditioner, and bed. I don't even need a TV."

"Oh, all our rooms got TV. They's two got broke air conditioners, but all the TVs work."

She took Jessica to one of the two units in the back, away from the road.

"Now, you shower, get cool, and sleep all you need. You can pay later. When you want coffee, just come up front and help yourself. It's there day and night, and I'll see you get a real cup, none of them plastic things."

Jessica took the key from her. "Thank you," she said, smiling.

Closing the door behind her, she sank into the bed and closed her eyes. Minutes passed before she felt strong enough to kick off her shoes. Finally, she stood, pulled down her panty hose, tossed them onto the TV. She stepped out of her dress and removed her bra.

In the bathroom, she adjusted the shower to a steamy warmth and turned her back to the nozzle so the pulsing stream drummed on the muscles of her neck and shoulders. Now, in the steamy embrace of the shower stall, her body grew limp. She turned, lifting her face to the spray and fully surrendered.

At first she sobbed silently. Her shoulders trembled. Finally she wept aloud, hands pressing the sides of her face. She cried as children do.

When she stepped from the shower, she felt emotionally drained. Opening the suitcase, she removed a peach-colored satin robe, tied it securely around her, walked unsteadily to the bed and dropped onto it. Turning on her side, she clutched a pillow to her breasts.

If she'd been traveling a fraction slower, she thought, it would have been over—that might have been so much better.

———

Jessica awoke feeling weak, but rested. She dressed slowly, in gray tennis shorts and blouse and white leather sandals. Sighing, she stepped out into the late afternoon.

After paying for the room and sipping a cup of coffee, more to please the manager than quench thirst, she walked along the beach, allowing the warm breeze and clean fragrance of the sea to empty her mind. I won't think about anything important now, she thought. Not today, maybe not tomorrow. Yes, I'll think. I'll do a lot of thinking. When I feel like it, not before.

But when she returned to the motel, she took from her suitcase a pen and notebook and went to the tiny patio behind her room. She sat at the wrought iron table, and wrote:

The gods are toying with us, Peter. I came to the island to discover some isolated spit of sand where I might learn how to spare you pain and loneliness, and to make whatever sense I can of it.

But the gods will have their fun. *A bridge falls out from under me!* That close! What are the odds of that? One in a billion? That close to being spared the pain, terror, slow disintegration. But it was only the gods toying with me, like little boys amusing themselves by plucking the wings from flies.

Even now I tremble. Were you here, I'd cling to you, draw your strength to me, the firmness of your flesh and close embrace. But you make that impossible, Peter. *I* must be there for *you*—*I* bringing *you* solace.

I would rather be alone.

Usually the writing helped to focus her concentration, objectify the problem and alleviate the pain. But that afternoon she felt no resolution, no peace, so again she sought to put it out of her mind. Although she had little appetite lately, she walked to the Isle Dauphine Restaurant, high on a bluff overlooking the sea, a vast stretch of sand and blue-green water. Children frolicked in the foamy surf along the beach. Far to the west, the sky was turning red and orange, with streaks of purple.

The restaurant was busy and animated. Waitresses dusted velvety peach-colored chairs, replaced aquamarine tablecloths with fresh ones, and neatly folded white linen napkins. Classical music played over hidden speakers.

She ordered a Caesar salad with chunks of grilled chicken and ate slowly. Maybe I'll have a beer, she thought, but wondered whether wine would be more appropriate, or a Brandy Alexander. What was a woman dining alone expected to drink after dinner? Brandy in a snifter, perhaps. Certainly not a Bloody Mary or beer.

She ordered the beer.

After a second glass, she felt herself drawn to other diners, although none seemed to notice her. She smiled for no reason. A waiter smiled back. I'm drunk, she thought, almost laughing aloud, intoxicated with freedom and beer and the miracle of being alive.

At dusk, she walked back along the beach to her room, watched an hour of television, took another shower, swallowed some pills the doctor had prescribed, and went to bed. By then the beer's effect had worn off. Her sleep was tortured with nightmares, horrible wreckage, blood-streaked faces, amputated limbs, falling, falling...

———

Through much of the night, the eerie white glare of floodlights from Coast Guard cutters, helicopters, the Sheriff's flotilla, even a fireboat from Mobile, illuminated the water surrounding the bridge. To the north, state troopers and county patrolmen had cleared the long string of cars from the bridge. Although the sirens had ceased wailing, alternating flashes of red and blue gave a freakish animation to the shadows.

Large cranes on barges continued into the night lifting chunks of bridge debris from the water and dropping them into hopper barges. When filled, they were pushed five miles into the Gulf where another crane unloaded them, creating an artificial reef.

Along the channel, to the east for several miles and to the west almost to the Mississippi River, shipping lanes grew congested with backed-up traffic.

By then, a giant tug named *Big Betsy* had raced down from Mobile pushing an empty barge and carrying officials from the Alabama Highway Department. After a quick inspection, they gave approval, and debris was lifted from the coal barge to the empty one. Divers fastened chains around the submerged car, and the crane lifted it. Finally, with the channel relatively clean, *Big Betsy* used her four thousand horses to push the partly submerged barge out from under the bridge and to the south of the channel, where it was anchored.

———

A few minutes before midnight, Lou Parrish returned to his Pelican Pub with an empty ten-gallon coffee pot. Even at that hour, every strand of his artificially colored golden hair remained sprayed in place, and his T-shirt and Spandex shorts had been changed three times—after each shower—to keep them fresh. At 32, he seemed more the professional athlete and model of his former years than the dilettante entrepreneur he'd become. Yet, this Monday night, Lou decided he looked a decade older than he had the day before.

Since mid-afternoon, he'd been running free coffee and sandwiches up to the bridge, for volunteer crews. Now, with the effort finished for the night, and yellow warning lights flashing from vessels in the channel, Lou Parrish called it quits and invited his friends back to the Pub for a nightcap. Randy Manning, Al Reed, and Norman Whitney were already sitting at an oval table on the second-floor deck.

A slight breeze from the west made the night pleasant. The men were gazing silently at the dark, brooding water when Lou climbed the steps. He put the coffee pot on one of the empty tables, stretched, and yawned.

"What'll it be, guys," he asked wearily, "Ginger ale for Al, and beers all around?"

"You know I'm on the wagon," Randy said. "Ginger ale's fine."

"Beer for me," Norman said. Sweat had stained his white shirt. Grime and wrinkles marred his new trousers.

"Coming up," Lou said and went inside.

"Three years now, right?" Al asked.

"Three years," Randy answered. "How about you?"

"Ten and holding. Look, Randy, if I didn't know better I'd tell you to have that beer after all, 'cause I got bad news. Don called. He quit this afternoon as of immediately."

Randy leaned back, locked his hands behind his neck and stretched.

"On a bender?"

"Nope. Says he got another job, driving that Ruth Knebles around. You know her, the one with the big black limousine. Stays all summer out there at Seaview."

"Well," Randy said and shrugged. "I went through hell kicking that shit," he said. "There ain't enough bad news in the world to get me drinking again."

Zechariah Ledbetter, in his late sixties and proprietor of the island's only general store, the Ship to Shore, lumbered up the steps. White haired and fully bearded, he resembled an Old World sea captain, although he had never been on the water much because, as he admitted freely, he feared it.

"Guess you're gonna have to settle down and get some work done, Manning," Zach growled.

"Just worry about your store, Ledbetter," Randy replied.

"I been worrying about my store forty-five years. Did a damned good job of it, too."

Lou returned with a tray full of cans and bottles.

Zechariah took a beer and nodded gruffly. He looked out across the sound, at the distant lights of Coden and Bayou La Batre. "Well, there's not much to count on in a place like this," he mumbled to no one in particular. "Not the weather. Not many people, that's for sure, wouldn't you say, Al?"

Both natives of Dauphin Island and the old village, Zach and Al had grown up friends. When Al announced he was leaving the island for a job with the oil rigs, Zach cursed him for abandoning the place—and Zach.

"It's desertion is what it is, Al Reed. Just go on with you then."

"I'm trying to better myself, Zechariah, which you would be happy for me for if you was any kind of true friend." For a while they neither spoke nor wrote. But Al lost an arm in an accident on the rig and came back to the island. After twenty years, they mellowed.

"That I would, Zechariah," Al said, leaning his head back on the bench and studying the stars. "People here always coming and going, running from something—the law, a wife and kids, bill collectors. Or maybe running *after* something—the beach, mostly, I guess, the sun, getting lucky and having somebody besides yourself to make love to for a change." The men laughed.

"Now, don't make fun of Al," Lou urged with mock seriousness. "After all, at least when most of us get bored, we can switch hands." Again the men laughed. Smiling, Al held up his hook.

The night grew still. Finally, Al mumbled, "But there's some things you can count on, and some people, too. When things get tough, they'll be there, even if they don't like you much. Nothing special about it—that's just who they are. It's what's in 'em."

"You know, Al, you're right!" Randy announced. "And here's a toast to one of the most dependable guys I know: Norman Whitney!" He looked at his ginger ale, and touched it to the other men's bottles.

"To Norman!" the men cheered.

"Thanks," Norman responded without expression.

"He was out there carrying barricades, moving people, running errands. Look at the guy! Coast Guard thought he was a victim, wanted to airlift him to a hospital. Look at him!"

The men chuckled. The once white dress shirt hung unbuttoned from Norman's shoulders to reveal a sun-pinkened chest. Stubble darkened his face. Hair fell limply over his forehead.

"He don't look much like a college professor to me," Zechariah Ledbetter grumbled, staring at the deck and shaking his head.

"That he don't," Al agreed. "He's a pitiable sight, he is."

Randy finished the can of ginger ale and stood. "Might as well get to bed, I guess," he said. "It sure ain't gonna be any slower tomorrow. Norman, be here by six in the morning. We'll get your car out first thing.

"Bet it'll be a year before they get that bridge fixed," Al said.

"So how the hell am I supposed to get stock for my store?" roared Zechariah, throwing his arms wide in exasperation.

"Go back to the same thing we did before they built the bridge in the first place, I guess," Al said.

"Pull the ferry from Fort Morgan and run it to Bayou La Batre four or five times a day, you think?"

"I don't know what else there is to do," Al said. "We got a couple thousand people here on vacation. They sure ain't gonna stay a year. This guy here," he pointed with his hook to Randy. "He'll probably set up water taxi service. He ain't got enough to do. Of course all the females ride free, long as Randy gets to ride, too." The men laughed.

"Well, we can laugh now," Zechariah, grumbled. "But I got a feeling. This summer's too damned hot and humid. All that heat out there in the Gulf and Caribbean, that don't bode well."

"You talking about a hurricane, Zechariah?" Al asked.

"All I'm saying, it don't bode well."

Randy slapped Lou Parrish on the back. "You're a good man, Lou. Thanks for the ginger ale. In fact, thanks for what you been doing all day. It's really been one hell of a day."

"You might say that," Norman muttered, patting some beer on his sunburned face.

"Come on," Randy said to him. "Let's get you back to the motel. You need your beauty rest."

When the others were gone, Lou stood next to Al on the deck of his Pelican Pub. Both men leaned against the rail, facing the sound.

"You don't get no Academy Award for acting tonight," Al said. "All them smiles. I saw through it, no trouble. You want to talk about what's got you so glum?"

"Nothing to say," Lou mumbled. He gestured toward the lights surrounding the bridge. "That says it all. My life's over. I'm out of business." He turned and began cleaning off tables.

"It ain't gonna be so bad," Al said, putting his hand on Lou's shoulder. "We'll talk about it in the morning."

———

Thirty minutes later, Norman Whitney stepped from the motel room shower and examined his body in the mirror above the dresser. His sunburned face had a haggard look. His eyes were sunken, his shoulders slumping. During the entire day he hadn't eaten a single meal, and now his stomach growled.

He ignored the discomfort, stumbled to the bed, collapsing into it. For a moment, he lay on his back staring at the ceiling and reflecting on the events of the day. He shook his head, and burst into laughter. Rescuing people sure is a hell of a lot tougher than teaching philosophy, he thought. With the sound of his own laughter playing in his head and a vision of himself jogging naked along the shore that morning, Norman fell asleep.

TUESDAY

CHAPTER V

Against the steel gray of the pre-dawn sky rose the jagged silhouette of the bridge like a fractured prehistoric skeleton. The air was still and silent. Here, in this transcending hush of night to day, was a timelessness that made the pristine western end of the island, the still water of the sound, and the leaping, frothy waves of the Gulf a single whole.

From the pine grove in the old village south of Manning's Garage, where the natives of the island lived, came the sound of a squeaking hinge. A dog several houses away heard it and barked. Doyle Donahue stepped out of his home and closed the door behind him. He didn't bother to lock it. None of the natives did, and it wouldn't matter anyway. He turned west and walked across the grass to the corner, then south along the dirt road, clutching a coiled rope in his hand. His pace was neither quick nor leisurely, but steady in an awkward, limping stride. One after another he passed the tiny houses of white clapboard and cedar shakes and a few of brick, homes of friends and neighbors he'd known all his life, their kids' bicycles and beach balls sheathed in morning darkness. He passed the brown clapboard house where Zach Ledbetter lived with his wife, and the white clapboard house where Al Reed was born and raised, the one he sold when he left the island. A young Creole couple owned it now. On his return to the island, Al had bought a place nearer the beach.

From the opposite side of the street, a shaggy brown mutt trotted up to a wire mesh fence and growled.

"Oh, be quiet, Barney," the man said. "It's just old Doyle. Just old Doyle." The dog whimpered.

The man continued on to Bienville Boulevard and across the road. On the other side, he turned east and moved along the shoulder, staring thoughtfully at the grass before him. Why ain't they come for me by now? he wondered. Why didn't they come and get me? So deep was his reverie, he didn't see the black Cadillac limousine pulling out of Hernando Street a block away. He gave no thought as it approached and passed him, Don Long at the wheel, Ruth Knebles next to him. Both waved, but Doyle never looked up.

At the bird sanctuary, he turned south into the woods and continued along the sandy path he and his friends had taken as children. All around him, tall and dense, were loblolly pines, yucca, and saw palmettos. Here, as a youngster, he'd hidden in the thickets.

"Ninety-nine, a hundred. Ready or not, here I come!" Remembering, he shook his head.

What did he have to show for thirty-four years of life? In a month, he would have made the final payment on the tug. Then he could have used those monthly savings to fit out *Barbara* as a proper ship. He could have bought a swing meter like the others had to tell him when he was moving out of the channel. Some even had radar. To start the *Barbara*, he had to run below deck and kick the engine over by hand like a Model T. He could have installed an automatic starter. And insurance—he'd have gotten that, too. As it was, they'd sue him and he'd never own anything for the rest of his life. And those people on the bridge who'd died because of him. He cursed himself.

The path ended abruptly at a large old water oak. A ranging expanse of undulating sand draped in morning glory and pennywort vines lay before him. A quarter-mile beyond, the blue-green water of the Gulf touched the sand with silver tongues.

Doyle turned to the oak. The wood rungs were still nailed in place. He uncoiled the rope and tossed it up and over a high branch, and, with the help of those rungs, climbed to the first limb.

He sat for a moment to gaze out on what he'd always known was the most beautiful view in all the world. Although the sun hadn't yet risen above the horizon, its color reflected from the clouds, painting the sea pink against the rich blue of the sky. Half a mile offshore, gulls already circled the Sand Island lighthouse. From here, it seemed the world belonged to him.

Finally, he stood, leaning back against the trunk, the rope still dangling from the branch a few feet above his head. He tied a loop in one end and slipped the other through it, pulling it tight around the branch. He made another loop, a large one, at the other end, and secured it around his neck.

He had thought about it all through the sleepless night. He had killed innocent people, God knows how many. He could never face the world again with that guilt and shame hanging over him. The right thing would have been to drown himself, but he knew he would lose courage and swim to safety once he began choking. And even if he went to the eastern tip of the island, by the fort, where the riptides were so savage swimming was forbidden and still a few people drowned every summer, he would hate the terror of choking, the feel of water in his lungs. A bullet might damage his brain and not kill him. Slitting his wrists was a woman's way, and would take too long, and besides he hated pain. He'd have taken pills if he'd had them, woman's way or not.

Then he'd thought of this tree, and the view, and suddenly he understood the end fate had ordained for him. He would not dangle at the end of the rope suffering a slow death, but drop far enough to snap his neck. It would be over instantly, painlessly.

He made sure the knot was at the back of his neck behind his left ear, and stepped out onto the limb, his eyes fastened on the horizon. Terror filled him, making his knees weak and his tongue thick. He could hardly breathe he was so afraid. Yet, he had killed others. He had seen them fall to their deaths. His life was over. He had no future, no reason to live. He didn't want to face another morning.

Just as the first gleaming edge of the sun appeared, he stepped off.

———

At the same time, not far to the west along Bienville Boulevard, Jessica Lofton walked past the room next to hers just as the door opened. Norman Whitney stepped out.

"Good morning," he said.

"Hello," she replied without enthusiasm. She walked past him.

"I wonder—you aren't going past the Isle Dauphine Restaurant by any chance, are you?"

She stopped walking, turned to him. "Yes. That's where I'm going." She began walking again.

"I ask because my car's at Manning's garage waiting for the muffler to be reattached, and I thought—I was too busy yesterday to eat. I sometimes forget things like eating. Right now I'm ravenous. I was wondering if you could give me a lift."

"My car's at Manning's, too," she said, "what's left of it."

"Norman Whitney," he said, extending his hand.

"Jessica Lofton." She smiled briefly. "The restaurant's not far. Why don't we walk?"

"All right. I must say, I've had the most miserable luck this week. The first morning, I drove out to the west end and got stuck in the sand. That's how I met Randy. He pulled my car out with his tow truck, but we ended up ripping the muffler and tail pipe off. He just got the replacement parts in yesterday, before the bridge went out."

"You want bad luck? Some of *my* car is in the Mississippi Sound!"

"You're kidding! Were you involved—"
"Yes!"
"Not the red BMW?"
"Yes!" Her eyes grew wide. "That's my car! So you understand why I can't give you a lift. I was almost killed! Were you ever almost killed?"

"Let me see. No, not that I remember."

The two strolled west along the grassy shoulder of Bienville Boulevard.

"Then you weren't. It's something you don't forget. First you're giddy with—well, joy. You laugh aloud. It's like you've done something naughty and gotten away with it. A minute later, you're sick with fear. You came that close to being dead forever."

"And I thought *I'd* had a rough day," Norman said. "A brush with death puts things in perspective."

Half a mile farther west, Ruth Knebles and Don Long sat at a table in the Isle Dauphine Restaurant and watched gulls glide over waves.

"I could just sit here and look out the window all day," Ruth said, her face reflecting contentment. "I guess it's a sign of old age."

"You're not old," Don said, lifting her hand and patting it. "I appreciate the job, you know. To tell you the truth, it's a lot easier than the garage."

Ruth frowned. "It might not be easy as you think," she said somberly. "You gotta take care of me. Remember that. You're my bodyguard, not just a big shot driving a Cadillac."

"I know that," Don said. "You know I do."

Norman and Jessica stepped into the foyer. He led her to a table along the window, next to Ruth and Don.

Ruth turned in her chair to stare at Jessica through squinty eyes. "You're the one!" she said, pointing.

"I beg your pardon?"

"You're the one just got across that bridge by the skin of your teeth. You were in that little red car!"

"Oh—yes," Jessica said, smiling.

"I was in the black Caddy!" Ruth exclaimed, as though meeting a long lost friend. "I'm gonna go to mass sure as hell come Sunday. That was a miracle if there ever was one, you and me right on the edge like that."

Norman chuckled. "It's *all* a miracle," he said.

Ruth's frown became a smile. "Come, come sit with us," she said, motioning them toward her with both hands. She stood and pulled out the two remaining chairs at the table. As Jessica and Norman took the proffered seats, Ruth glared up at Norman.

"Who are you?"

"Norman."

"He's the one I told you about," Don said. "Remember the guy got stuck out in the sand?"

"This is him?" Ruth slapped the table. She shook her head in disbelief. "You can't drive a car in loose, dry sand," she told him.

"I know," said Norman dryly. "It was wet and hard from the rain. The sun quickly dried it out. So who are *you*?"

"Ruth Knebles," she answered curtly, then added, for Jessica's sake, "This is Don Long."

"Jessica Lofton." She extended her hand to Ruth and Don. "Norman and I are staying at the Bluebird." As an afterthought, she added, "In separate rooms, of course. We just met." Everyone laughed.

"Norman who?" Ruth demanded.

"Whitney."

"So, what do you do for a living?"

"I teach philosophy at a small college in Pennsylvania. You've probably never heard of it. I hope I can finish writing a book here this summer."

"You a writer?" Don asked, his face brightening.

"Yes, I've written a few books."

"What's this one about?" asked Jessica.

"A philosophy of sex."

"Hmm," Ruth growled. "If you ask me, you're not supposed to philosophize about sex, you're just supposed to *do* it." Again they laughed.

"I agree wholeheartedly. Incidentally, I heard you two were quite heroic yesterday, along with Randy Manning."

40

The scowl vanished from Ruth's face. She beamed at Don. "He's the bravest man I ever met."

"Aw, stop it—you're embarrassing me." Don buried his face in his arms.

"Here, order yourself a big breakfast," Ruth said, handing Don the menu.

She turned to Jessica. "How long you down for?" she asked.

Jessica began to speak, but her voice trailed to silence. She stared through the window to where the sea met the horizon, her face drained of color. "I don't know," she said. "I'm almost afraid to make plans after yesterday."

Ruth took Jessica's hand and squeezed it. "Well, I guess I'm just lucky—it scared the hell out of me right then and there, seeing that bridge disappear right before my eyes. Do you know what I did? You can ask Don—I went back to the condo and looked in the mirror and said to myself, 'You was almost a dead person, Ruth Knebles.' And then I said, 'But you're not, not even a scratch. A miss is as good as a mile.'"

———

Across Bienville Boulevard from the Isle Dauphine Restaurant, Randy Manning sat with some friends around a table at Milt's Diner. It was a small, crowded place, four tables with red and white checkered plastic table cloths, a counter, and four stools. Cookie Manning, Randy's wife, reached between him and Al with a steaming pot of coffee and refilled the cups.

"Eggs-coming-up-in-a-minute," she said so rapidly and with so heavy a Korean accent that it seemed a single word. She smiled at Randy and vanished.

41

"Doyle's ass is in real trouble now." Al told the men sitting at the tables. He turned to Lou Parrish. "I slept on that cot in the garage last night—why walk home, it was so late anyway? So this morning, it must've been five o'clock, I hear this motor. I go out for a look, and there's a Marine Police cutter pulling up next to Doyle's tug. I'm telling ya, they tore it apart. Didn't find but a case of empty beer bottles and one whiskey bottle—also empty."

"Doyle wasn't in the boat?" Randy asked.

"Nope. In fact, when they seen me standing there, they come on over and say, 'You know who owns that boat?' 'Doyle Donahue,' I says.

"'Where is he?' 'I don't know where he is,' I tell them, 'What I know is, he owns that tug.'"

"They're gonna throw him in jail," Lou said. "It's crazy. When he's sober he's a crackerjack on the water—the best."

"They gotta catch him first," Al said.

"Well," said Lou, staring at the table, "I don't know why or how he did it, but he sure screwed up my business."

Randy shook his head. "An Army Corps of Engineers guy told me last night they don't know if the bridge is worth rebuilding."

Randy saw the strain in Lou's face. "Lighten up," he told him. "Look on the bright side of it."

"What bright side?"

Everyone was silent until Al said cheerfully, "There *ain't* no bright side!"

"Look," Lou said, slapping his hand on the table, the color rising in his boyish cheeks, "I've got my life savings in that place, and a mortgage that could sink a battleship."

"Your life savings, boy?" Al said, his voice soft, but his squinting eyes riveted on Lou. "You're a fool if you let that worry you. Do what you can and forget about the rest. Now, you can't survive selling booze to the local crowd. You gotta sell something else, something every last one of them might want, and then you gotta publicize it—fast."

Lou leaned forward and cupped his chin in his hand. "Like what?"

"Like shrimp on the barbie!" Al suggested, bouncing with enthusiasm. "Like a fish fry! Like a clambake!"

"We don't have clams in these waters," Randy said.

"Well, then—an oyster bake!"

"Yes," Lou said thoughtfully, "Yes! I can get them fresh from the islanders before they head over to Bayou La Batre. I'll run off flyers this afternoon—Joe Dingman has a photocopy machine at his real estate office." He rose and started for the door, mumbling to himself. "Yes, good idea. Thanks, Al."

———

That morning, two thousand miles southeast of Dauphin Island, at the extreme eastern end of the Caribbean near Grenada, a large patch of water began to stir. Throughout the spring and early summer it had lain dormant, a one-hundred-square-mile eddy in the North Equatorial Current. While all around it the water continued to flow, dissipating its heat to the cooler depths, this one patch, week upon week, had absorbed the scorching heat of the sun until even bottom feeding creatures a thousand feet below felt the change. At the surface, the water temperature rose above ninety degrees Fahrenheit, several degrees higher than the surrounding current.

On that Tuesday, a mass of cool, heavy air drifted from the snowcapped Andes in Ecuador, moved through the Magdalena chain in Colombia and settled over the Caribbean. The North Atlantic trade winds collided with this dome and veered slightly north from their east-to-west pattern. The winds tugged at the ocean currents beneath them, altering them as well, and that hot eddy slowly began flowing northwestward.

CHAPTER VI

After breakfast, Jessica returned to the motel, slipped into a forest green bikini and headed to the beach. Norman meandered through the back lanes of the old village toward Randy's garage. He walked with his hands in his pockets, gazing at the ground and planning the chapters of his book. Periodically he would stop, staring straight ahead, consumed with a fresh idea. The natives who peeked through their curtains watched and whispered of the stranger who stood motionless, staring at nothing.

When he arrived at Randy's garage, Norman found the gates unlocked, the doors wide open. He sauntered past the garage to the yard, intrigued by the great variety of junk Randy had accumulated.

Since arriving at the island, Norman had devised a plan. Staying at the motel all summer would be both expensive and stifling to one who loved the out-of-doors as he did. He would buy a used boat, keep it in a slip on the Mississippi Sound or a nearby bayou, and have the world spread out before him.

Of the three useable boats in Randy Manning's yard, one was of particular interest, a twenty-four-foot black and white Fiberform cabin cruiser named the *Alicia B*. It had a V-bottom with a sharp chine, and so much freeboard Norman had to search the yard for a ladder to scale the gunwale.

Finally he climbed the rungs and stepped over the rail into the cockpit, a five-foot by seven-foot space with a built-in fiberglass bench and holding tanks for bait and fish. Forward, a glass door opened to the pilothouse, the captain's chair and controls on the left, stairs on the right leading below to a galley with a tiny sink, stove, refrigerator, a table and two bench chairs that converted into a bunk. Forward of the galley were a large V-berth, a head, and plenty of storage space. Large portholes offered a ranging view of the junkyard.

It was exactly what he'd hoped for when he'd begun daydreaming during those Pennsylvania blizzards the previous winter.

Randy's tow truck skittered into the yard just as Norman climbed down from the *Alicia B*. Blackie, Randy's big Lab, leaped from the truck's bed and raced toward him with low, ominous barks, its tail wagging. Reaching the man, Blackie leaped up, rested its paws on Norman's shoulders, and licked his face.

"Yuck," Norman responded. "Hey, Randy, what's the story on this boat?" He pushed the dog down.

Randy stepped from the truck, the rusty hinges squeaking, and slammed the door.

"Some guy swapped it for a car I was selling four years ago. It's a piece of junk."

"Looks okay to me. What's wrong with it?"

"Well, nothing exactly," Randy said, striding over to Norman, "but it must be twenty-five years old, and that fiberglass is brittle, especially in this hot, humid climate."

"Does all that stuff in there work—the stove, refrigerator, sink and all?"

"Yeah, but—"

"How much do you want for it?"

"Oh, hell, I don't know," Randy said, scratching his head. "It's been sitting here forever. Sure you want it?"

Norman's eyes brightened. "It's like a dream!" he said. "You can't imagine how much I was hoping to live on a boat. Tie up somewhere private, peaceful, with a view. Maybe do a little fishing. This would be perfect."

"Yeah, I can imagine," Randy said dryly. "The second happiest day in a man's life is when he buys his first boat. The first happiest is the day he gets rid of it."

"I know, I know," Norman said, laughing.

"How's five hundred sound?"

"I'll write the check now. How soon can you put it in the water for me?"

"Might as well do it now, I guess." He strode quickly across the yard to the office.

"Al," he said as he entered.

"Randy, where the hell you been?" Al answered. "It's a full-time job just answering the phone around here, everybody complaining, wanting their work done, asking where you are. What am I to tell them?"

"Norman just bought himself a boat. We're gonna launch the *Alicia B*. It'll only take a minute. Give me a hand."

"God almighty," Al answered. He continued mumbling to himself while following Randy to the truck. Randy started it and backed the truck to the trailer of the *Alicia B*. When the cup on the hitch hovered directly above the ball on the tow bar, Al yelled, "Hold it!" He cranked the handle of the rusty trailer gear until the socket dropped onto the trailer ball, then pressed down the latch, put the bolt through it, tightened the nut, and fastened the cross chains to the shackles.

"Take 'er away!" he yelled as Norman jumped into the truck next to Randy.

"Where are we launching it?" Norman asked.

47

Randy moved the through-the-floor transmission stick into low-low, and crept forward. Creaking and groaning, the trailer shuddered and lurched out of its ruts.

"We ain't got but one choice," Randy answered. "Billy Goat Hole's way east—no sense going all that way. A couple miles west there's Heron Bayou. Used to be a nice house back there till a hurricane got it. The ramp's still in great shape. There's even a dock to tie up at."

They pulled out of the yard onto DeSoto and began gathering speed. "Maybe we should check the tires," Randy said. "And you might want to put some fuel in the tank."

"Good idea. What's it take?"

"It was made for leaded. You'll have to use the highest octane."

"No problem."

Approaching the corner, Randy turned into the station and carefully maneuvered the boat's transom close to the pump. Norman approached the attendant.

"Fill it up with the best you've got," he said. Smiling, Randy shook his head. He stepped out of the truck and added air to all four of the trailer's tires.

Twenty minutes later, Norman joined Randy in the truck, a somber expression on his face. "I didn't know it was a sixty gallon tank," he mumbled. "Where is it, anyway?"

"In the bilge, under the galley."

"Oh. And the engine?"

"Engine?" Randy turned the key, started the truck, and shifted into low-low. "Ain't no engine. Why'd you think you got it for five hundred bucks?"

"Oh." Norman rested his chin in the palm of his hand and pondered. As the truck led the trailer in a wide swing to the right and started south toward Bienville Boulevard, Norman asked, "Then why did we buy sixty gallons of gas?"

"'*Course* there's an engine, right under the stern deck. An inboard-outboard, a real bastard to work on. And expensive as hell to fix. They're always breaking down."

"Oh," Norman said, smiling. Then, somberly, "Oh." But his concern vanished quickly. Leaning out the window, he felt the warm breeze wash his face. It carried the smell of fresh-mown grass and honeysuckle.

Overhead, a line of gray clouds blocked the sun.

At the stop sign across from the water tower, Randy brought the truck and trailer to a halt. Again he took the turn wide, and was half way through it when Norman heard a loud "pang," and a few seconds later another. Looking through the truck's rear view mirror, Randy saw the boat listing sharply to the right.

"Damn," Randy said. "Damn!"

"What?"

"The axles. That trailer's as old as the boat. They snapped like twigs. It was that sixty gallons of fuel. I should've known better."

Both men got out and walked around the trailer. Not only had both axles broken—the sudden weight on the right wheels forced them to splay outward. The *Alicia B.* seemed to hang precariously over the lower right side of the trailer.

Immediately a crowd of onlookers gathered. Traffic began to back up in all three directions of the intersection.

"You're gonna have to get that thing out of there, you know," one driver yelled after blasting his horn.

"You really think so?" Randy yelled back. "You stupid shit." The man drove away.

"What are we going to do?" Norman asked plaintively.

"Well, Frank Jackson has a brand new heavy-duty trailer in the yard. Of course, his boat's on it. I'll have to put it in the water. We'll see if Jake Martin can come over from the marina with his forklift and..." Randy's voice trailed off.

His hands clasped behind his back, Norman walked the length of the trailer gazing forlornly at his boat. He turned and, staring at the pavement, shuffled back toward Randy, looked into the man's eyes, and offered an ironic smile.

CHAPTER VII

At noon, Jessica returned from the beach, where she had been thinking, watching gulls and listening to waves gurgle along the shore all morning. She slipped out of the forest green bikini, showered, and put on white knee-length shorts, a short-sleeved blouse and tennis shoes. Her shoulder-length hair had a natural soft wave, and a few strokes of a brush enhanced its rich ebony sheen. She decided against makeup.

Locking the motel room door behind her, she sauntered along Bienville Boulevard. Waves of heat rose from the asphalt. Only a steady breeze from the Gulf made the afternoon tolerable.

When she reached the parking lot of Milt's Diner, she paused. Across the street the beach stretched for miles. Youngsters in colorful bathing suits darted along the water's edge to vanish in midday haze.

She turned back to the diner. A large sign in the window declared, "Barbecue spareribs. Best in Alabama. $4.95." Someone had crossed out Alabama and written, "The World!"

Cookie Manning greeted her: "Hello, hello! You sit where you like it, okay?"

"Thank you. I'll sit at the counter, I think."

"No want table?"

"No, this is fine."

Bottles of jalapenos at ten cents apiece, pickled okra for the same price, and homemade beef jerky for a dollar cluttered the imitation marble counter.

"You like menu?" Cookie's round cheeks lifted in a radiant smile.

Jessica smiled back. "I want those best-in-the-world, even Alabama, spareribs."

"Ah," Cookie exclaimed. "You hit bull's eye!" She turned to one of the pots behind her and began stirring.

"No customers at this hour?" Jessica asked.

"Fishermen to market, Bayou La Batre," Cookie said, turning politely to face Jessica while she talked. "Some home in shade. They get up early, sleep now. Eat late. Only dumb tourists go out in sun, get heat stroke, burn skin. Oh, my big mouth—I no mean you."

"You're right," Jessica said, laughing. "Does any other animal on the planet actually *want* to be burned by the sun?" She leaned across the counter, as though sharing a secret. "My mother-in-law visits the French Riviera twice a year just to tell the bridge club where she got her 'lovely' tan. Fact is, I could make a football of her jowls."

Cookie laughed heartily, her voice delicate. She put a plate of spareribs in front of Jessica, along with coleslaw and a stack of paper towels, and said, "My name Cookie, short for Korean nobody can say."

"I'm Jessica, Cookie! Glad to meet you." She extended her hand. Cookie grasped it and shook it in a manly way, grinning broadly.

"What you want drink?"

"Ice tea, unsweetened, with lemon please."

Returning with the tea, Cookie asked, "You buy house here?"

"No, I just needed to get away for a few days." She took a rib in her fingers, and, heedless of the sauce she smeared on her face, sank her teeth into the meat.

"God, these *are* good!" she exclaimed.

"Good, yes?"

"Great! I bet they *are* the best in Alabama—probably the world!"

"You married," Cookie stated, pointing to Jessica's ring.

Jessica nodded, her mouth full. She sipped some tea.

"Yes," she said. "Oh, no—I didn't need to get away from *him*." She saw the puzzled look on Cookie's face and the gentleness in her eyes.

"Actually, I *did* want to get away from him. I *had* to." She bit into another rib. "No need to get into the gory details."

"He have girlfriend?"

"Oh, no—he's..." She continued gnawing on the bone. "I could use a little support, some understanding. Instead, I think he *blames* me. One minute he's crying, the next he's hostile." She sighed. "Why am I telling you this? I don't even know you."

They laughed. Cookie touched Jessica's arm.

"Men silly, sentimental, weak," she said.

Jessica nodded. Willing herself to be cheerful, she licked her lips and rolled her eyes. "Boy, this is fun," she said, biting into another rib. "I mean, letting it all out. What about you, Cookie. Are you married?"

Cookie dropped her eyes. "Yes," she said shyly. "Randy Manning my husband. We meet in South Korea, 1975. He with U.S. Army—soldier since war. I love him. I beg him marry me. He bring me back with him to U.S.A. as wife. We go here, we go there. He work sometimes. I work sometimes. He restless, always drinking, twelve cans, twenty cans every day."

"Beer?"

"Yes, beer. He get in fights, get arrested, have car accident. He go to jail whole year." Cookie glanced down at the floor, her face somber.

"Does he still drink?"

"No! Not one drop three years. He go AA. He keep busy always. No time for drink." She turned toward the sink. "No time." She ran water onto the dishes.

Jessica finished the spareribs and wiped most of the sauce from her hands and face with paper towels. Cookie brought her a damp cloth, and gently wiped Jessica's cheek clean. "Use for hands," she said.

"Thanks." When her fingers were clean and dry, Jessica took the American Express card from her shorts pocket and placed it on the counter.

"Oh, Jessica," Cookie said, giggling with embarrassment. "We no take credit card. Just money."

"How thoughtless of me. Well, let me leave my wristwatch as collateral—I don't have my wallet. I'll be right back with the money."

"Don't be silly," Cookie said harshly. "Wristwatch not necessary. Money not important. Trust important. Friendship important."

Their eyes met. Jessica took Cookie's hand in both of hers. "What time do you close?"

"Today Tuesday—seven o'clock."

"I'll be back by then, or tomorrow morning for sure."

————

Stepping out into the boiling humidity, Jessica decided not to go back to the motel immediately. Cookie's words had unsettled her. This stranger had reached to Jessica, offered friendship. She could still see Cookie's eyes, the longing in them.

She turned west toward the uninhabited end of the island. Walking along the road, her hands folded behind her, she kicked at the crushed oyster shells beside the shoulder. When she came to a sandy, tree-lined lane leading to the sound, she meandered along it. Soon she reached a concrete ramp that disappeared into the muddy ripples of Heron Bayou, half an acre of deep water leading to the sound.

She sauntered to the retaining wall, took off her tennis shoes and socks, sat on the weather-beaten wooden plate, put her feet over the side, and twitched her toes in the water. A few feet below, on the silt bottom, two hermit crabs moved slowly along, wearing large white snail shells.

Across the bayou, a blue egret stood motionless on one foot, almost invisible against the green and brown cattails.

Jessica lay back in the grass, her hands behind her neck, her feet in the water, and watched the sun duck in and out behind gray clouds. She basked in the joy of simply breathing, of being alive.

The rain fell quickly, in large, noisy drops. They felt warm against her face.

———

The weather pattern on Dauphin Island during the summer is monotonous in its predictability. Each morning, the sun heats the air and water over the gulf, sound, and bay, and that warm air, absorbing moisture like a sponge, rises lightly through the heavier, cooler atmosphere in lazy, spiraling undulations. By mid-afternoon, usually around three or four p.m., it reaches high into the troposphere, where its heat dissipates, its moisture condensing. From the island, that moisture appears as black clouds racing in from the horizon. They approach swiftly, a battle line attacking the island.

———

At the intersection near the water tower, neither Randy nor Norman noticed the darkening. They were busy slipping pads between the prongs of the forklift and the hull of the *Alicia B*.

———

From the highest dune west of the bird sanctuary, the movement of clouds and rain were a drama. When the black line first formed, cool air began to tumble invisibly up the beach and rustle through the tops of trees. Gray streamers of rain broke through the blue sky at the horizon and fell to the sea.

Approaching the beach, the streamers merged into a single sheet of gray. Torrents of rain pummeled the waves, and gusts now reached the shore. The army of raindrops marched over the beach, across the dunes. They pelted wild vines and palmettos. They fell through the leaves of the old live oak, and splashed on Doyle Donahue's face.

He blinked twice and stared through puffy, glazed eyes at the silvery crests of waves in the Gulf. At first he was aware only of the sledge hammer-like pain in his head. With every heartbeat, the ache seemed to pass through his body to his toes. He tried to swallow; his throat burned like fire.

Minutes passed. He didn't try to move. Even his eyes seemed fixed. Where am I, he wondered. Am I dying? Dead? He dropped his gaze to discover himself in a sitting position, his legs stretched out, his shirt and pants stained with the muddy blur of dry blood. Still he didn't understand.

He struggled to lift his right hand, to feel his face. Another pain shot through his shoulder. No doubt he was dying, but where and how? Slowly he turned his head.

"Oh," he moaned. Must've broken my neck, he thought. With his left hand, he touched his throat. He felt a rope, followed it with his fingers to the knot behind his ear. Then he remembered. Everything. The drunken stupor, the morning on the sound, the bridge, the cars tumbling, the unearthly screech of metal, the night of sobriety, the early morning walk to the beach, climbing the tree, the rope, jumping. A profound depression overwhelmed him. He had no right to be alive. He couldn't even kill himself right.

He touched his face. It was puffy and caked with blood. He lay his hand tentatively on top of his head. There, the blood was still sticky. He rolled his eyes to the right, and saw in the sand the dead limb, the rope still tied around it. So it was the limb and not his neck that had snapped. And when he'd hit the ground, the dead branch had hit him.

"I'm not dead after all," he mumbled through swollen lips.

In spite of the screaming pain in his shoulder, he reached both hands to the rope around his neck and forced it loose. He noticed the rope burns in the palms of his hands, and when he tried to move his feet, he realized both ankles had been sprained. Could he have reached up at the last instant and grabbed the rope?

I must look awful, he thought. He'd try to make it back to Al's cottage. Al never locked the door. No one on the island ever did except the tourists. He could wash up, maybe put a towel around his head, sleep. He'd had no sleep to speak of in two days, so tired he couldn't think straight.

He rolled over and got on his hands and knees in the sand. He dragged one of his feet under him, then the other, and, supporting himself against the trunk, stood. His swollen ankles throbbed, but supported his weight. He took a few cautious steps away from the tree, along the path through pine woods toward Al's place.

———

At the height of the downpour, Zach Ledbetter left the general store in his wife's care and hurried to the intersection to see for himself the cause of the commotion. Now he announced with authority to a couple of dozen onlookers, "It just ain't gonna work. The boat's too heavy. It'll dump the lift!" Like the others, he was soaked to the skin, and squinted to keep the water out of his eyes. But the rain was warm and refreshing, and, in the monotonous life of the island, a trailer with two broken axles in the middle of the busiest intersection constituted entertainment.

"You're forgetting something," Randy told Zach and the others. "That's Jake Martin up on that fork. All by himself he weighs as much as that boat!" The crowd laughed.

"Yeah, yeah," Jake said dryly. "Except old Zach there might have a point. And I'm telling you now, I'm not responsible for anything that happens." He turned to Norman. "You got that?"

"You're not responsible," Norman agreed. He turned to the crowd. "He's not responsible."

Randy studied Norman and shook his head. "You're a pitiful sight, old buddy," he said. "You've got the eyes of a beagle and the mane of a sheep dog that fell overboard. You want to sit in the truck?"

"I don't mind the rain. In fact, I like it."

"All right, let's get this show on the road," Randy said. "Jake, bring the fork in slow now. A little lower. Hold it! To the left. That's good. A little closer. A little closer. Stop. All right, bring up the fork. That's it. You got it now. A little more. It's clear of the trailer! Now just hold it there. Don't do anything. And for God's sake, don't get off the lift!" The crowd laughed again.

Randy ran to the truck, already re-hitched to the broken trailer. He dropped the transmission into low-low, and slowly dragged the metal wreckage out from under the boat, wheels and axles screeching and clanging against the asphalt. Slowly it moved out of the street and onto the grass, the axles digging trenches in the dirt.

When the truck stopped, Norman unhitched the trailer. Randy spun the wheel and backed to the good trailer, where Norman secured the ball in the cup. A moment later, Randy had the trailer backed perfectly under the boat. Jake lowered the *Alicia B.* onto the rollers.

"I appreciate your help," Norman yelled up to Jake. "What do I owe you?"

"Hell, I'm not taking any money from you," Jake boomed, backing the forklift. "What if some of your bad luck rubbed off on it? I'd be in heaps of trouble!" He waved and sped away.

———

Slowly, patiently, Randy drove the truck and trailer along Bienville Boulevard through the downpour. They passed the motel, and, half a mile farther on, Milt Goldberg's diner. A block beyond that, he swung wide to the right, and headed toward Heron Bayou along the sandy lane.

As he approached the ramp, the rain abruptly ceased. A woman rose, as though from the water, her hair matted in wet strings, a saturated white blouse clinging to her ample breasts like another skin.

"It's Jessica Lofton," Norman exclaimed. "Do you know her?"

"Nope. I'd remember a body like that."

"She's the one who owns the red BMW in your garage."

Jessica recognized Norman, waved, and approached the truck. Norman got out.

"You got caught in the rain?" he asked.

"I loved it!" she answered, her eyes wide and sparkling.

"I'm gonna turn this rig around," Randy said. "Just keep out of the way."

Norman stepped closer to Jessica. "Shouldn't you be getting out of those wet clothes?" he asked. He studied with candor the outline of her body, the spring-like freshness of her damp face.

"Oh, I'll dry off soon enough," she said. She had gathered her long hair and was twisting it like a cloth, wringing the water out of it. "And *you*!" she exclaimed. "Don't you own anything but white dress shirts, brand name trousers, and Florsheim shoes?" She began laughing.

"Curiously, I don't—no, not a single pair of jeans. When I'm in public I dress like a professor. Privately, I don't... well, I don't dress at all."

Jessica dropped her head back, her face to the sky, revealing an elegant neck. "It must be nice to be that comfortable with yourself," she said.

When Randy had the trailer on the ramp, he called to Norman: "See if you can climb up there on the trailer tongue and get hold of the bow rope. Make sure it's fastened to the bow cleat. When I back the trailer down, the boat'll float off. Just hang on to the rope and walk it up to the wharf."

In the sky to the north and west, patches of dark clouds still blocked the sunlight. Yet, beyond the bayou with its cattails and wiregrass, the Mississippi Sound glowed in sunlight.

This'll be the view I awaken to each morning, Norman thought. It's paradise.

He held tight to the bowline, watched his boat as water surrounded the stern, caressed the hull, crept toward the bow. As though taking on a life of its own, *Alicia B.* floated free from the trailer. With little effort, he led the boat to the wharf.

Using a hitch knot, he bound the bowline to a cleat on the wharf. He found the stern line inside the boat, and fastened it to another cleat.

Randy came running from the truck with an armful of fenders.

"These'll keep the boat from hitting the wharf," he said, tying the fenders to the pilings.

Norman stepped back to where Jessica was standing. "That's my boat," he told her.

"It's beautiful."

"I'll be able to watch the sun set from the cockpit."

"It's a lovely, lovely spot. So quiet. I thought I'd stay just a few minutes, and I've been here since lunchtime!"

Randy approached. "Look, I gotta get going," he said. "Come on, I'll give you a lift."

"Thanks," Jessica said, "but I think I'll walk back. It's just down the road."

"How about you, Norm?"

"I'll keep Jessica company."

"Sure enough. Oh, by the way, Norman, I got your car fixed today. You can pick it up anytime." Waving, Randy drove off.

"Dear Lord, what am I thinking?" Jessica exclaimed. "I can't be seen in public looking like this—soaked to the skin, my hair a mess, barefoot. I can't even put my shoes back on—look at my feet!"

"They're lovely."

"I mean the mud!"

Norman chuckled. "Tell you what," he said, sitting in the grass and untying his own soggy dress shoes, "I'll take my shoes and socks off, too, and walk in some mud. Then we'll both be barefoot and muddy."

"You don't have to do that," Jessica said, blushing.

"Ah, but I want to. I love feeling grass under my feet."

"Me, too! I grew up in the country—we went barefoot all summer."

"You lived on a farm?"

"A small one, twelve acres, mostly wooded, a barn, a few chickens for eggs. We never ate them— the chickens, I mean. Two goats to keep the grass and weeds down. And give us milk. Oh, the milk. The *milk*! We had goat cheese, goat sherbet, chocolate goat milk. We had to milk them twice a day. Dad had a rule: My three brothers and I had to drink goat milk three times a day. And still we could never use it all. We ended up giving it to neighbors, passing out quarts of it at church Sundays. It won't keep, you know. It's great when it's fresh, but after a couple days, goat milk really tastes—goaty."

"I'm a city boy myself," Norman said. "Born and raised in Philadelphia. I like living in Center City. You can walk to everything. Never a dull moment—sirens, gunshots, theater openings. Give me either a big city or somewhere wild and all alone, like the west end of this island. What I really don't like is the suburbs. They're just so suburban."

Jessica laughed lightly.

The cicadas were beginning their evening songs as the two continued along. Shadows stretched across the grass.

"That's exactly where I live, Peter and me—and his mother. In the suburbs of Mobile. Nice suburbs, but that's what they are. Oh, if that woman—Peter's mom—saw me now, she'd screech, 'Don't you have any self-respect, Jessica Lofton, soaking wet and bare feet in public?'"

"Self-respect hasn't a thing to do with bare feet and soaked breasts—blouses, soaked *blouses*, I mean."

Jessica blushed. They grew silent, staring at the wet grass as they sauntered along.

Finally, Jessica said, "We should have a christening party for your new boat."

"When?"

"Tonight!"

"I'd love to, but tonight I need to buy some shorts—these slacks are definitely inappropriate—get my car from Randy, pack my stuff, move out of the motel into my boat, and perhaps finally—*finally*—kick back and relax. How about tomorrow night?"

"Tomorrow, then."

CHAPTER VIII

Cookie Manning drove up to her husband's garage in the red Cadillac he'd given her soon after he'd opened the place. He'd done some work for a man on Little Dauphin Island Bay and took the car as payment. He'd overhauled the engine, sanded and puttied some rust spots and dents, and spray painted the whole body. On their tenth anniversary he'd given the car to Cookie. It was sixteen years old.

Now she drove it everywhere, her head high with apparent pride, and kept in her heart the secret of her embarrassment over such ostentation.

She stepped from the Caddy into the warm early dusk. The horizon to the west was a strip of blazing crimson, the sky abutting it deep purple and black. Above the garage, Cookie saw a scattering of stars. Randy would be hungry by now. She gathered the bags and thermos and headed toward the office in the front part of the garage.

"Goddamn it, Randy, that car's been in here three weeks for a lousy tune-up." It was the thundering voice of Mr. Wentworth on Iberville Drive, across from the Shell Mound Park. Cookie had met him a few times at the garage. "God knows I've been patient, Randy, but there's a limit. You swore it would be ready today."

"You're right, Bert. What can I say? First, Mrs. Stout's husband got sick. I think it was a heart attack—we still don't know. Had to get him to the hospital in Bayou La Batre. Then that old couple on Conti Street, the Epsons, needed freon in their air conditioner. They'd die in this heat. Then the bridge gets knocked out—I been working on that day and night…" Cookie saw the frustration in her husband's face. "It's one thing after another," Randy said. "Now how am I supposed to get parts?"

Bert Wentworth threw up his hands and turned away from Randy. "It's just excuse after excuse," he said. "The bridge has been out two days. This car's been here three weeks."

Unobserved, Cookie quietly slipped into the garage, where Al Reed was picking up tools, putting them back in drawers and hanging them on walls. It was a part-time job, sweeping and cleaning up when he wasn't on the water with Doyle Donahue. Now, it was his *only* job. Maybe he'd finally be able to keep up with the mess.

"Hello, Al!" Cookie announced. "I bring chicken tonight, and mashed potatoes and peas!"

"Hi, Cookie," Al said with enthusiasm. He stopped what he was doing and wiped his hands on his work pants. "You shouldn't've gone to the trouble."

"No trouble for you, Al. Come, sit down."

Amid the chaos of clutter was a single island of neatness in the northwest corner of the garage, next to the office door. Here, two plywood walls formed a tiny room containing a sink and toilet. On the outside of those walls were a cot, a table, three chairs and a refrigerator.

Al and Cookie sat down at the table. She opened one of the bags, put a plate, fork, and knife before Al, and withdrew two bowls. From another bag she unpacked the food.

"Help yourself," she told him. "Plenty food. Eat what you like."

"You don't have to tell me twice," Al said, beaming. "Here, you take some."

"No, no. I eat already." She watched Al help himself, and smiled in satisfaction. Finally, she asked, "Why Randy no fix Mr. Wentworth's car?"

"Well," Al began, avoiding her eyes," he's too damned good-hearted." He ripped a large piece of flesh from a thigh and chewed silently. Finally he said, "He's always doing for others, like he thinks he's some kind of boy scout. Somebody needs help, he drops everything and runs. Me, I'd say, 'You wait your turn.' Not Randy. And the crazier it is, the quicker he goes. Last week some lady's cat was up a tree. Damned if he didn't take the fire truck and get it down. Took half the day. Me, I'd say 'Stupid cat got up there by itself, let it get down by itself!' A few days before that, a call comes in on the radio, some guy's motor quit out in the Gulf. He gets in that boat of his, goes out and tows him back. Three hours, and what does he charge? Ten bucks."

They were silent. Bert Wentworth's booming voice resounded through the cement block walls.

"Where is Don?" Cookie asked. "I bring him chicken, too."

Al chuckled. "Old Don Long won't be needing your chicken, Cookie. He got himself a real plum job. He's driving for this rich old bag from Mobile. Just up and quit without notice. That's what the island's all about, you know."

"I know," said Cookie. "I know what you mean." She thought for a moment. "So, who helps Randy now?"

"I guess just me. Nobody else looking for work that I know of."

With a final blast of profanity, Wentworth slammed the outside door of the office. Cookie could hear him striding across the oyster shells to the road.

The inner door from the office opened and Randy stepped into the garage. He looked haggard.

Cookie rose. "I bring good food," she said. "Chicken, mashed potatoes, peas, coffee. You come here, sit down." She went to him and led him to the table, pulled out the chair for him. Exhausted, Randy sat. Cookie took the muscles of his shoulders in the palms of her hands and kneaded firmly. Randy closed his eyes and moaned. Her strong thumbs massaged the muscles of his back. She could feel them relaxing. He dropped his head forward.

After a moment, she bent to kiss his neck. Abruptly, she straightened and walked away, her back to him.

"What's up?" Randy asked.

For a moment she didn't answer. Finally, she said, "You have perfume, you have perfume. Marwick woman perfume." She spun on him. "It true! You go with lots of women. What wrong with Cookie? You don't want me? You don't love me?"

Randy rose and spread his arms. "No, Cookie, there's no one—"

"No lies! No lies! Be a man, tell truth!"

He turned from her, staring down at the plate of food, and sank weakly back into the chair.

"Oh, Randy," Cookie cried. She turned and ran to the red Cadillac.

Al took a few more spoons of mashed potatoes, which he particularly enjoyed. Then he rose and started for the office door.

"I'm gonna sleep in my own bed tonight, Randy," he said, and walked through the office and out into the street, shutting the door behind him. He watched the Cadillac speed into the distance.

Randy stood alone in the garage.

He was in the same spot several minutes later when Norman Whitney ran into the garage. He found Randy staring into the untouched plate of food on the table next to him.

"Randy, I can't believe it," he gasped. "My boat—it's sinking!"

———

For a moment, the early sixties rock music blaring from the Pelican Pub across the street from the garage distracted Al. He felt the old rush of excitement the music, booze, and beautiful women once brought him.. But he turned away, shaking his head, and meandered west along the wharf. He'd had all that, especially after the oil rig accident that had taken his arm. All the liquor he could find the space to store. Nothing but the best—Beefeater, Glenlivet, Dom Perignon, wines older than he was with names he couldn't pronounce. An eight-hundred-thousand-dollar settlement buys a lot of good booze.

It bought him a Mercedes, too. And that Bluebird Motel on Bienville Boulevard where Norm had stayed. It bought him cocaine and all the other shit, and there wasn't a night he went to bed without two women to keep him warm and happy.

But he was always driving to New Orleans or Atlanta instead of running the motel. And even though he'd hired Randy to keep it clean and rented, Randy never seemed to get around to it. He lost the Mercedes in a poker game when he put it up against a yacht, and all of a sudden there wasn't enough left to pay the mortgage on the motel. One day it was all gone—the women, car, motel, money, drugs, good booze—everything gone, except the addictions. Some church group sent him to a rehab center in

Florida for three months, and he came back a little smarter, able to look himself in the mirror again without disgust. He'd lost his arm and what did he have to show for it? Well, he thought, a lesson. Call it an education.

Finally after working and saving for five years, he was able to buy himself a house. He walked along the edge of the wharf, the music so distant now it was lost in his reverie. Below him, he saw a school of tiny, luminous fish, and from far out in the bay, he heard the horn of a freighter heading toward Mobile. Against the black water of the sound the green and red buoy lights flashed in four-second intervals. Far across the sound, at Cedar Point and Coden, the street lights gleamed like rows of fluorescent yellow beads, the tiny headlights of cars passing beneath them.

Al took the humid night air into his lungs and released it in a long, contented sigh. The money hadn't bought any of this. This had been his from the beginning. He turned and started along the lane south toward the loblolly pines and old village.

A small crowd had gathered at the Pelican Pub. On the dance floor, Abby Marwick, her full breasts and buttocks straining the seams of her red bikini, gyrated to the tune of "Knock Three Times." Three men in their late teens and early twenties surrounded her, clumsily imitating her movements and applauding in rhythm.

"That's it—shake it, honey!" one yelled.

"Oh, yeah!"

"You're driving me nuts, baby."

Abby laughed. She raised her hands over her head and shimmied her breasts, moving close to each man in his turn, brushing her pelvis against his. When she reached the last man, the youngest, she locked her hands behind his neck, and pressed her lips to his, watching his eyes widen.

"Yeah, man!" one of the others shouted. Abby lowered the man's face to the crevice between her breasts. "Lick me," she told him.

"Oh, God!"

In the darkened northwest corner of the bar, Ruth Knebles and Don Long had moved their chairs side by side and sat facing the sound and holding hands. Don gulped a draft beer from a mug, and Ruth belted down a double scotch on the rocks.

"There's one!" Don said, pointing to the sky above Bayou La Batre. Ruth had challenged him to find a falling star.

"Where?" I can't see it with all the reflections from the lights in here. These bifocals don't help, either."

"Hey, Lou!" Ruth bellowed over the music. "Yeah, you. Any other Lou in here? Two hamburgers with the works, another beer and double scotch."

"Coming up!" Lou yelled.

Ruth allowed her arm to flop over Don's shoulder. "Now we gotta get a bit serious for a minute," she said, her words beginning to slur. "I don't want you worrying or nothing, but I got a call this afternoon, while you were out buying groceries."

"What kinda call?"

"From my husband, the rug man." She had mentioned him several times to Don, always as "my husband, the rug man."

"What'd he want?"

"He said he don't give a damn if I get a divorce—goodbye and good riddance. Offered me a hundred thousand bucks, take it or leave it. And you know what he says? He says, 'You can't win a settlement suit when you're dead.'"

Don stood abruptly, turned and, mouth open and eyes bulging, studied every face in the room. There were no unsavory-looking strangers. Trembling, he lowered himself into the chair again.

"Lou!" Ruth shouted. "Cancel the drinks and bag the burgers. Get them here snappy." Turning to Don, she said, "Don't you go worrying now. How the hell are his thugs gonna get here, assuming he's so damned stupid to try a thing like that when everybody knows I'm divorcing him?"

"How's he gonna get here? By boat. By plane. By ferry. If they want to bring a car so they can drive around, see the sights after they're done killing us dead. One ferry's been going back and forth from Fort Morgan all day, and they just started running another one to Bayou La Batre three times a day. I think we better clear out of here."

"Oh, pshaw," Ruth said, dismissing his concern with a few flicks of her hand. But Don saw her somber expression.

Lou Parrish moved across the dance floor toward Ruth and Don in long, gliding strides. He had the build, posture, and face of a youthful Charlton Heston, and when he passed Abby Marwick, she placed both hands on the skin-tight shorts covering his buttocks and squeezed. He stopped, switched the tray from his right hand to his left, put his arm around her, pulled her to him and kissed her deeply. The crowd roared its approval. Abby laughed, watching the churning muscles move away from her.

"Be still my heart," she said, putting the back of her hand to her forehead. She stumbled to the bar and sat on the nearest stool.

"Two hamburgers with the works," Lou said, handing Ruth the bag.

"Here." Ruth took a twenty-dollar bill from her purse. "Keep the change."

"Well, thanks!" It was the first genuine enthusiasm Lou Parrish had felt all day.

"Leets get out of here," Ruth told Don.

A moment later, Don unlocked the passenger door of the limousine and helped in. Just as he opened the driver's side door, he heard a screech of brakes. A block away, a large gray car spun around the corner into DeSoto, heading for the cafe. Don jumped into the car, slammed the door, and started the engine.

"I think we're in trouble," he said as the vehicle squealed to a stop behind him, its headlights reflecting in the Cadillac's mirrors, blinding Don. He stomped the accelerator to the floor, and the car leaped forward, its rear tires spraying bits of oyster shells at the vehicle behind it.

The Caddy sped along DeSoto and slid around the corner onto Levert Street before the other car began to move, but it closed on the Cadillac at brutal speed. Don saw the headlights in his rear view mirror through a haze of dust from the dirt lane. Again he spun the wheel to the left, fishtailing into Bienville Boulevard. At Hernando, he swung a right and headed toward the beach.

"There goes a couple ribs," Ruth said, straining against the seat belt, not to mention the boobs.""

"They're gaining on us. I don't like it a bit."

The other car followed in his tracks, now not thirty feet behind.

"When we get to your place, I'm gonna hit the brakes," he told Ruth. "You jump out and get inside fast as you can. I'll hold 'em off. Leave the hamburgers. Get your key ready."

"I don't want you getting hurt."

"Me neither. Just do what I tell ya. Unlock your seat belt. Ready?"

As the Caddy approached Ruth's condominium, Don spun the wheel to the left and slammed on the brakes. The chase car swerved violently to avoid a collision.

"Go, Ruth!" Don yelled, opening his own car door. Ruth leaped out and ran toward the building.

"Okay, you bastards, come and get me!" Don shouted, leaping from the car. "Let's see what you got!"

The door of the other car opened. "What the hell's the matter with you, Don? All I want is a little help getting Norm's boat out of the bayou."

Randy Manning stepped from Norman's gray Thunderbird.

CHAPTER IX

Al Reed walked on his tip-toes in the darkness, determined to make no sound that might disturb the ghosts of dead Indians. They had dwelled here, right here in the old village between tall pines like those now obstructing the moonlight. Before Jesus, before Plato, before Moses, they had buried their dead not half a mile away, under those thirty-foot high mounds of oyster shells where LeMoyne ended at Bienville Boulevard. Now it was called Old Mound Park, with a wooden sign and everything. Couples walked hand in hand under the canopy of great oaks draped in Spanish moss, three-hundred-year-old trees growing up out of those mounds, nourished by those Indian bodies. But Al had never walked on those graves and never would, because he believed in the spirits and respected them.

On nights, like this, shuffling along in absolute darkness, he felt them close around him, and could swear to actually seeing their shapeless vapors. One night in particular, sober as a scallion, he had known an epiphany: three gray clouds against the blackness of the road, not twenty feet ahead. They'd frightened him at first, but when his heart ceased racing and his breathing grew normal, he simply stood motionless, studied them, staring at those still, silent patches of mist.

Finally, they seemed to settle closer to the ground, so Al squatted in the middle of the dirt lane, knees apart and legs crossed at the ankles.

No one actually spoke. Instead, something happened inside his brain. It was as though the soul of the island welled up in him—not the people, not the Spanish privateers of the 1550's or the French under Iberville in 1699. Not them, but perhaps the spirit of the bones—the mountain of bones, as Iberville described them, heads separated from bodies so that the explorer first named this place, this small piece of earth unique in all the world, Massacre Island. Not souls of the British who took the island from the French in the Seven Years' War, nor of the Spaniards, who drove out the British during the Revolution, nor of the Americans, nor the Confederates, nor the Yankees, all of whom flew their flags and played out their petty games like insects on the hide of Dauphin Island.

These were not the island's soul. Only the natives—and precious few of them—had seen its soul in thundering waves, howling wind, crashing timber, the fearsome eye of a strung-up shark and the ghostly movements of spirits in darkness.

That night, Al had become one with the spirits of the massacre and all the children of the land for all time. From then on, he felt their presence along the lanes of the old village, and sometimes saw their mist-like essences. His fate, insignificant in itself, grew cosmic in its union with the whole. Like the island, his form was encompassed in flux. He had lost an arm; the island had divided in two. He would decay; the original island had changed its shape and location a thousand times, and still it lived.

So lost in such thought was Al that he reached the door of his cottage not quite sure how he'd gotten there. He opened it, flicked on the light and started into the sparsely furnished living room when he heard, "Now, don't be scared, Al."

He screamed, leaping across the room.

"It's just me—Doyle," the tugboat skipper said. "Damn, I didn't mean to scare you, Al."

"Well, you sure did. You really sure did." Holding his hand over his heart, Al slouched to the sofa and collapsed. Doyle came and sat next to him.

"Al, I need a big favor," he said.

"I know you do. You busted the bridge. I was there, remember? Damn near got killed. Why'd you do that, Doyle?"

Doyle closed his eyes. His shoulders sagged forward, his chin resting against his chest. Al saw the tears in his eyes. "It was the booze," Doyle sobbed. "No, no excuses. I went down to get some aspirins. I left the pilothouse. I just really screwed up, Al. You know, I tried to kill myself this morning, and I couldn't even do that right. I tried to hang myself, and the branch broke. Can you believe it? Here, look at my neck."

Al saw the bruises and rope burns. He stood up and paced the threadbare carpet of his living room. Abruptly, he turned to confront Doyle.

"Yes, I can believe it," he said. "It's the spirits! You can't die. It's not the plan. I don't mean plan, exactly. It's not in the flow of things. You're needed."

"Where am I needed?"

"I don't know what I'm talking about!" Al declared in a frenzy. "I just know you have to live. It's essential. Some day you'll understand. Don't argue, don't fight, and for God's sake, don't try to kill yourself again. That's tempting fate."

Doyle pondered Al's words somberly. He held his chin in his hand and stared at the ceiling, then the carpet. "Well, I guess it makes sense," he concluded.

"In the meantime, you're gonna have to stay here," Al told him. "The island's crawling with fuzz out to put your ass in the slammer."

"I figured as much."

"You can have the couch. I'll get you a sheet. It's too hot for blankets."

A moment later Al returned with a pillow and a sheet. "Watch the TV if you want. Keep it low. I'm going to bed. Feel like I haven't slept in a year."

"Al, I think I'm gonna go for a walk now, it being dark out. I been sleeping all morning, since that branch knocked me cold."

"Yeah," Al said, and went to bed.

———

The door to Cookie Manning's house opened. She stepped out into the muggy darkness. During the five years since Randy had built that house, it had seemed to Cookie a miracle. In Korea she'd never dreamed one day she'd have a house of her own. Yet, Randy had built it, and had given it to her, actually put it in her name, after working so hard, usually alone, for months on end.

The old-timers like Zach Ledbetter had scolded Randy bitterly for building on a slab, right on the ground, behind the highest dune on the island. That dune had been built by the winds and storm surges of long-forgotten hurricanes. They'd piled countless thousands of tons of sand from Gulf beaches against the timberline, forming dunes half a mile long, and this one forty feet high.

Most people concluded Randy was crazy to build that close to the water—and doubly so for putting his house on a slab rather than pilings. "There's sure to be another hurricane," they said. "We average one every ten years down here. One good wave and that shack'll end up clear across the island in the Sound!"

Every time someone told him that, Randy just smiled.

She loved her home, but on this night, she could not bear to stay there. She left it, and stood for a moment with her back to the closed door like an animal escaping its cage, staring into the pitch black of the woods across the street and the starry sky over the dune.

"Oh, Mamma," she cried.

She ran along the winding walkway lined with the petunias, geraniums, violets, and snap dragons she'd planted, ran sobbing across the street to the path over the dune. Even before she reached the crest she was crying aloud, the sound merging in a curious harmony with the crashing waves.

"Oh, Mamma," she wept. "Oh, Mamma."

"Cookie?" Doyle was leaning against a slash pine about twenty feet closer to the water and to Cookie's right. He had thought to keep silent when he first heard her approach, but the pain and abandon in her weeping took him out of himself. She grew silent except for the sniffling.

"Who there?"

"It's me, Doyle Donahue."

"Doyle? Oh, my God, you in big trouble."

"I know." He came to her and sat near where she stood. "I wish I had died."

"No, you should not say such thing." She sat next to him. "Life is wonderful gift."

Doyle turned to her and tried to see her face in the darkness. He saw only the silhouette of her profile—small nose, high cheekbones, broad forehead, short hair. He had always admired Cookie for her simple beauty and cheerfulness. "That's strange, hearing you say that," he said softly, "seeing how miserable you are. If you want somebody to talk to, I can listen."

A sob caught in Cookie's throat. "Oh, Doyle, you have such big problem, you have no room for Cookie's."

"Yes, I do," he responded eagerly. "I was spared today, and Al says there's a reason. Maybe it's just to listen." He wanted to tell her he never took for granted her smile when she served him breakfast at Milt's Diner. It was probably the best way in the world to begin the day. Instead, he kept silent.

"Randy never have time for me," she said softly. "Ever since we come to U.S. we always move. Get work in California, not happy. Texas, not happy. Jacksonville, the same. He work all day, out all night. I think he has other women. Sometimes I *know*. But he always come home to sleep with me. He tell me he love me, take me to movie sometimes. I am raised to honor husband, to worship him. So I keep silent. I give him freedom. I live to make him happy, nothing else."

She began to sob again. Her whole body shook with it, and Doyle's eyes grew wet. He put his arm around her shoulder, pulled away, and rested it around her again.

"Cookie," he said. "Cookie." He spoke her name softly.

"We come to island. Everything okay for a while," she said. "Then I smell the perfume, and sometimes he not even come home, say he have to tow car out of ditch, rescue boat, but I know. Why Randy make me so miserable?"

For a while, they were silent, listening to the waves in their hypnotic monotony of whoom and ahh, whoom and ahh. Together, they watched a freighter far out in the Gulf moving toward the bay.

Finally, Doyle said, "You know, I'm not very bright, Cookie. Ain't nobody gonna argue with me on that score. But I do know a couple things, and one is, Randy ain't making you miserable, any more than liquor made me a drunk. I'm the only one could make me a drunk—not another person on God's earth could have done it. Just me. And nobody's making you miserable but you. And nobody can make you happy but you. You gotta understand that, Cookie, 'cause you're just too fine a woman to be crying like this."

He reached up and felt for her face and brushed away her tears. Cookie took his hands in hers, and in the darkness pressed them to her lips. "Thank you, Doyle," she said. "You are good man."

Now, Doyle thought, maybe I can die.

––––––

A couple of miles to the west that night, in the bungalow next to Abby Marwick's home, Betsy Smith knelt beside her twelve-year-old son Joshua and her six-year-old daughter Sarah.

"Dear Father," she prayed, her folded hands resting on the boy's bed, "thank you for all the good and beautiful things you've given us—the puffy white clouds, the smell of flowers, the taste of peaches and strawberries, music. Lord, teach us to not take for granted your bounty. Joshua," she whispered, "tell God what you're thankful for."

"Lord," the boy prayed, "thank you for baked macaroni." Betsy suppressed a smile. She nodded toward Sarah.

"Thank You, God, for Mommy and Daddy."

"And, dear Lord," Betsy said, "thank you for this wonderful vacation. Bless Daddy and Abby for making it possible."

"And God bless everyone in the whole world," Joshua added.

Sarah scrambled into her bed against the wall. Betsy kissed her on the forehead. "Tell me a story!" the child pleaded.

"I don't want any dumb stories," Josh said. He was already in bed, facing the wall, a pillow over his head.

"Leave the light on," Sarah pleaded.

"No, it keeps me awake," Josh said.

"I'll leave the door open, sweetie," Betsy told her daughter. "The hall light'll shine on your side of the room."

"Goody."

Betsy walked over to Josh, lifted the pillow from his head, and kissed the boy's cheek.

"Ugh," he responded. Betsy smiled.

"Getting too old to be kissed by your mother?" she asked. "I love you."

"I love you too, Mom. Now, can I go to sleep?"

Betsy walked through the living room and out onto the deck. Her husband Bill stood at the rail watching a freighter creep along the dark horizon. To the west at some distance, Abby Marwick's home was dark.

Betsy put her arm around Bill's ample waist. "Pretty humid," she said. "Wonder if it'll rain."

"TV says we might get some rain later in the week," Bill said.

"Is it sore?"

Gingerly he touched the top of his bald head. "A little. I put the ointment on."

"You have to wear a hat when you're out in the sun. I told you that."

"Just stop nagging. I can't very well swim with a hat, can I?" He shook his head in disgust. "Shucks," he said, as though uttering a profanity.

"All right," Betsy said. "I apologize."

Bill shook his head once again, then faced his wife and smiled. He pulled her close to him, and turned his attention again to the distant freighter. "Sometimes don't you just wonder what it would be like to cut loose, get a job on one of those things, sail off somewhere so different it would be a whole new life?"

Silently, Betsy told herself she enjoyed her life very much the way it was, and had no desire to travel anywhere, much less to strange and distant places.

After a while, she stood on her toes and kissed Bill's round, fleshy cheek. "I'm worn out," she said. "I'm going inside."

"You need vitamins."

"What I need," she said, leaning her head against his shoulder, "is to check the kids into a kennel for a week and take a *real* vacation."

At five hundred dollars a week during the high season, the beach house had been a good bargain. Actually, Abby had offered the house free to Betsy and Bill, but Bill had growled, "We're not a charity case!" So Abby had agreed to take the money—and to put it into a college fund for the Smith children. The wooden bungalow was tiny compared to Abby's fortress. But it was more than adequate with two large bedrooms and a single great room-kitchen-dining room area with an unobstructed view of the Gulf to the south and the Mississippi Sound to the north. The furnishings were inexpensive but adequate, except for the inordinately squeaky bed. Betsy particularly liked the great room with its plush brown corduroy sofa facing the color TV that had been bolted to the corner walls.

Yawning, she turned it on and stretched out on the sofa.

John Brent, meteorologist for WALF, was saying, "Weather reconnaissance aircraft are reporting a minor tropical depression in the Caribbean, two hundred miles southwest of Jamaica, with winds gusting to twenty-eight miles an hour. For those of you who track storms, this one is moving to the northwest toward the Yucatan Peninsula at twelve miles an hour. It's at sixteen degrees latitude, eighty degrees longitude. According to the National Oceanographic and Atmospheric Administration, the depression is expected to keep on its present course, making landfall by tomorrow morning, when it will undoubtedly deteriorate."

"Undoubtedly deteriorate," Betsy repeated, her eyes closing. "Indubitably, indomitably deteriorate."

WEDNESDAY

CHAPTER X

It had started out as a patch of unusually warm water drifting lazily westward with the surrounding current, releasing heat and moisture into the air. When that column of warm air reached several thousand feet, it cooled, its moisture condensing into huge, puffy white cumulus clouds.

Nothing more might have come of it if those clouds hadn't collided with the cooler easterlies.

In a matter of hours, several events occurred. The cooler, heavier wind of the easterlies rushed toward the lighter, warm column of air as though into a vacuum, compressing it on all sides. Like water flowing from a large hose into a thinner one, the hot, moisture-laden air shot upward at ever increasing speed.

That wind rose high into the troposphere, now black with the moisture of cumulonimbus clouds—thunderheads. A vast area of thunderstorms raged, winds beating the waves to scud, driving the rain. Lightning leaped from cloud to cloud and slashed the sea.

Just before midnight Tuesday, an hour after Betsy Smith fell asleep on the sofa, the National Oceanic and Atmospheric Administration upgraded the tropical disturbance to tropical storm Constance.

By dawn Wednesday morning, two facts became clear to those tracking Constance by plane and satellite. She was taking on a life of her own, fueled by an apparently fathomless supply of heat in the water beneath her. And she would not make landfall on the Yucatan Peninsula. During the night, she swerved north to eighty-six degrees longitude and twenty-two degrees latitude. Constance seemed headed toward Galveston, Texas, at speeds of twelve to fifteen miles an hour. Weather reconnaissance aircraft reported gusts of sixty miles an hour.

———

All over the island, people came together to discuss the storm. In front of the general store, a retired shrimper told an oysterman, "You wouldn't catch me in Galveston right now if my life depended on it. I was out in the Gulf when a hurricane hit one time, and I can tell you—"

"You tryin' a tell me you was at sea in a hurricane?" interrupted the oysterman.

"It was enough of a hurricane to scare the hell out of me, that's what it was, and it weren't even a hurricane. Winds sixty-five miles an hour—gotta be seventy-four to be a hurricane. I was so scared I prayed to every god I ever heard about—and them I didn't, just in case. Musta got through to the right one somewheres along the line, 'cause I'm still here to talk about it."

At Billy Goat Hole, some vacationing fishermen were making bets.

"Fifty bucks says it peters out before the eye reaches Texas."

"What makes you so sure?"

"That's cool water in the central Gulf there. Need warm water to run a hurricane."

"I'll take that bet. I say it's going south into Mexico where it belongs. What the hell's in Mexico that a hurricane's gonna make any difference?"

"I don't mind making a hundred bucks," said another. "I say it's coming in around New Orleans.

Good riddance to the French Quarter—
highest-priced slum on earth."

All three laughed.

"I'll tell you this, boys—if it lands in New
Orleans, we're gonna get pretty damn wet here."

On the public beach, two women reclining in
lounge chairs and watching their children play in the
sand shared opinions.

"My husband says we should get off the
island right away. This is the same guy wanted to sell
Chrysler when it fell to eight dollars. Did I let him?
No, I bought more! Today it's worth thirty-five.
Walk away from this house we paid a thousand
dollars a week to rent? Not on your life."

"My Albert says it's all show biz. These
storm watches and storm warnings—it's to boost the
ratings. I come from Kansas, and not once in my life,
with all the tornado warnings and watches, did I ever
so much as *see* a tornado."

At the gas station, post office, and Randy's
garage people gathered to talk. Those who had not
spoken for lack of a reason, others who had
quarreled and been distant, now came together for
the universally sanctioned purpose of discussing the
weather. They spoke of previous hurricanes,
typhoons, blizzards, monsoons, the unfathomable,
boundless energy of the weather.

Yet, they spoke of Constance casually, a
vague, distant curiosity.

"They said on the TV this one's hard to
predict."

"Hard to predict! The weather's *always* hard
to predict. When's the last time they got it right?"

"I'll be home and back to work in Chicago
before any hurricane gets up this far—what is it, a
thousand miles away?"

"Hurricane—it sounds cool, man!"

———

Betsy Smith, wearing a demure light-green one-piece bathing suit, stood in the shallow water of the Gulf. A fresh breeze from the southwest touched her with its sultry warmth. She ran farther out and plunged into the waves.

Most mornings during vacation she arose long before Bill and the children, hoarding those moments when she could be alone with her thoughts and enjoy just walking or swimming. Sometimes she would think. Often she prayed. Today, she would pray for her best friend, Abby Marwick. They'd been inseparable since childhood, Abby physical, funny, popular, wealthy, Betsy more bookish and thoughtful.

So many memories, Betsy thought, rolling into a backstroke. She recalled the day in high school when Cynthia something-or-other approached Abby in the hall and, ignoring Betsy, said, "I'm having a party Saturday night at my house. Would you come?"

"Well, that's one way to get the boys to show up," Abby said nonchalantly. "You inviting Betsy?"

Cynthia glanced at Betsy, then the floor. Finally, she turned back to Betsy. "I don't know how much fun you'd have, Betsy. See, we're gonna dance, might even get some beer. I just know how religious you are."

"Betsy's not as square as some people think," Abby said. "You know, it just isn't looking good for Saturday, Cynthia. Betsy and me—"

Cynthia's face brightened. "Betsy," she said cheerfully, "Won't you *please* try to come with Abby to my party?"

"Well, I…"

"I just changed my mind," Abby said dryly. "What time?"

Betsy rolled onto her back, floating and studying the clouds. She recalled the Friday nights she stayed over at Abby's huge home north of Mobile, sleeping in the most lavish of several guest rooms. (Abby tacked a small sign to the door naming it "Betsy's Room.") It had a ranging view of pastures, a pond, and grazing horses.

Saturday morning, Betsy awakened to the aroma of a coffee cake baking in the kitchen below her room next to Abby's. She stretched lazily, sat up and gazed out across the fields of flowing grass. Finally, she stood, slipped into her slippers and in her pajamas headed downstairs.

She found Abby in the kitchen working beside Mrs. Marwick, chatting about one of the boys at school.

" Don't let any of them get fresh with you," advised Mrs. Marwick. She was short, slightly stocky, with a beautiful face, a close resemblance to her daughter. Giving advice came naturally to her, and she offered it freely to Mr. Marwick and even Betsy. The girls often joked about it.

"She means well," Abby assured her best friend.

In the living room, Mr. Marwick played popular tunes on the piano.

"This is such a happy home!" Betsy exclaimed.

"Well, thank you, dear!" Mrs. Marwick replied. "Come, sit at the table and I'll bring your breakfast. Henry! Breakfast."

It included poached eggs on English muffins, milk, and a small bowl of fruit.

Later, they saddled two horses and road along the side of a brook.

In the afternoon, in Abby's room they practiced kissing so they wouldn't be inexperienced when the right boy wanted to do it.

"I think you're drooling too much spit," Betsy told Abby. "Wipe your lips dry."

"Yuck! Keep your tongue in your own mouth," Abby told Betsy."

"You're supposed to stick your tongue in his mouth—I read it someplace."

"Well, I'm not doing it unless we're married, and he gargles first."

Graduation night. Boring speeches. The two of them alone in their caps and gowns under the stars, Abby hugging Betsy tightly, saying, "You'll always be my best friend," Betsy replying, "I love you like a sister, Abby. No, it's more than that—like the best part of myself."

They laughed, their eyes moist.

Betsy moved into a breast stroke.

Mrs. Marwick's head rested lightly on the coffin's white satin pillow. She had the Tranquility Suite at the end of the first floor hall. Every Marwick who'd died in the past fifty years had been laid out in the Tranquility Suite. It was large, for the entire family and friends of the family; even those who had known Mrs. Marwick as a child attended the viewing.

The white wallpaper with silver crests and angels complemented the gray carpet. Large Victorian lamps with milk glass bowls reflected the light gently to the ceiling. Two soft floods illuminated the coffin and, beside it, arrangements of purple violets and white orchids.

Silently, hundreds shuffled up to the coffin, paused, moved on to Mr. Marwick and Abby, Betsy at her side. Some remarked that a woman so young and vital could have died of cancer so quickly, a year after her daughter had graduated from high school.

When Abby could no longer control her tears, she took Betsy's hand and led her out into the parking lot.

"I don't understand it," she sobbed. "I just don't. I don't understand it."

Abby cried for days. Even Betsy's constant presence did no good. Finally, her father took her to a doctor, who gave her an injection and prescribed tranquilizers.

Six months later, her father dead of a heart attack, Abby's face a ghastly mask of hopelessness, damp with tears, but no sound, no sobbing.

The morning after the funeral, Betsy went to Abby's house and rang the bell. It sounded like the chimes on a church organ. Minutes passed. Abby didn't answer. Betsy turned the knob, found the door unlocked, stepped inside. Abby wasn't on the first floor. Panicking, Betsy raced up the steps to Abby's room. She found her sprawled naked across her king-sized bed, hardly breathing.

"You can't do that to me!" Betsy screamed the day she brought Abby home from the hospital. "It would kill me if you did that." Clenching her fists, tears streaming down her cheeks, she pleaded, "Promise me you'll never try to kill yourself again. Promise me, Abby!" Abby promised. She kept the promise, and plodded through each day.

Eventually, Abby took a couple of the many millions she'd inherited and bought a classical Greek mansion in Spring Hill known throughout the south as Kendell Hall. She and Betsy saw each other several times a week, usually without Bill's knowledge, since he disapproved of Abby's lifestyle.

Kendell Hall became infamous in that sedate neighborhood for rowdy parties. Neighbors complained of naked orgies around the pool. Police responded to drunken skirmishes on the front lawn. Betsy avoided phoning her friend evenings; she knew she'd hear raucous laughter and Abby would slur her words.

Dear God, Betsy prayed. Oh dear, oh dear. Help Abby.

———

Jessica Lofton hadn't turned on the television or listened to the radio for more than a day and a half. She had made up her mind to withdraw from the civilized world, resign from the human race, become an island in the middle of nowhere, find a simple, splendid isolation where nothing mattered.

She awoke feeling weak but clear-minded. Donning lilac-blue slacks and blouse and comfortable walking shoes, she went first to the motel office and helped herself to a cup of coffee. Later, she meandered to LeMoyne Drive and headed north, toward the bridge. It was still barricaded, yellow and white sawhorses held in place by sandbags. A string of yellow lights flashed rhythmically. Scores of emergency workers wearing yellow hard hats directed crews to shore up support beams of the bridge. Huge cranes lifted chunks of debris from the coal barge and surrounding water, their engines groaning under the strain, and placed each load almost gently into awaiting barges. But beyond all the noise and confusion, Jessica saw, scattered in the distance, a score of tiny wooden boats motionless on the placid water, each with a single figure standing upright, scraping his tine along the bottom, lifting the prongs, draining off water, dumping oysters onto decks.

For no apparent reason she felt like crying.

Turning back along LeMoyne Drive, Jessica sauntered toward Bienville Boulevard. Abruptly she decided to march straight to the Isle Dauphine Restaurant. She increased her pace slightly, swinging her arms, shoulders back and head high, sucking the humid morning air deep into her lungs. She would slip into the rest room, dab perspiration from her cheeks and forehead, pat any loose hairs back in place, take a table and order herself the largest... But she had no appetite at all. At least she'd get half a grapefruit and some tea, even an English muffin. That would make the doctor happy, if she could keep it down.

Perhaps she'd meet Norman there. She imagined him sitting proudly on the deck of his new boat, his clear brown eyes scanning the sunlit water. Even now, hurrying along the roadside, she had to smile. "You're a paradox," she'd tell him. "I can't figure out if you're a sophisticated stoic or an innocent, gullible child."

Norman wasn't at the restaurant. The disappointment she felt surprised her. She left without taking a table, walked slowly along the driveway and across Bienville Boulevard to Milt's Diner.

The place was crowded, a few tourists sitting at the tables, a dozen men with scruffy fishing hats, tattered jeans and T-shirts milling around the counter. Several spoke boisterously above the din.

Behind the counter, a rotund man in his sixties with a full beard stirred the contents of a large pot on the stove. Beside him, Cookie poured water into the coffee maker. Jessica walked up to the counter and called, "Hello, Cookie!" The men parted before her.

"Hello, hello, Jessica!"

"Is this usual," Jessica asked, leaning over the counter toward Cookie, "all these people so early in the morning?"

Cookie laughed. "This *late*. They should be on water. They stay, talk about weather."

"It's a lovely day. What's to talk about?"

"Obviously you're not a TV fan," said the man stirring the pot. He spoke in a surprisingly high voice for one so rotund, Jessica thought. "Seems like there's a hurricane brewing off the Caribbean."

"Constance," Cookie offered.

"Yeah, Hurricane Constance." He came forward, extending his hand. "I'm Milt Goldberg," he said.

"Jessica Lofton," she replied, grasping the large, leathery hand. Only two round eyes and a small, smiling mouth protruded from the otherwise bearded face.

"Welcome, Jessica," he said. "Yeah, the weather, a war, a natural disaster—that's what it takes to get them piling into Milt's Diner. Say, what can I get you, young lady?"

"Grapefruit?" She wrinkled her forehead questioningly. Milt shook his head no.

"I guess—I'll take two eggs scrambled," she declared emphatically, "and toast with jelly and butter—lots of both."

"Coming right up!" Milt said, smiling.

"And," Jessica said meekly, "sausage—links or patties, I don't care!"

When Milt turned to the grill, Jessica reached in her purse and handed Cookie twenty dollars. "From yesterday, my friend," she said by way of explanation. With a delicate smile, Cookie took the money and went to the cash register. When she returned, Jessica said, "Keep the change, please. You haven't seen Norman this morning, have you?"

"Norman?"

"Tall, light beard, brown eyes, in his forties?"

"Yes, I see someone like that. He with Randy, long time already."

The talk in the diner was of previous storms and tall tales of heroics, outrageous destruction and loss of life. Jessica became absorbed in it. Among these strangers, she felt like a child again, listening to her father, grandfather and neighboring delta mud farmers gathered around the kitchen table exchanging yarns. Even their voices, this boasting and exaggeration, sounded the same. She could have invented a yarn herself—the car slowly sliding back over the edge of the bridge, leaping out just in time to cling to the raw concrete by her fingernails, lifting herself up by sheer strength.

———

Abby Marwick's eyes fluttered and opened to view through the patio door of her bedroom a placid Gulf of Mexico, a sky of puffy clouds and azure reaching to the horizon. She grew conscious of the TV playing in the living room, and the cool air of the ceiling fan caressing her nude body. Finally, she felt the warm flesh of the men at her sides.

"Bernie," she called to the great room, "bring me coffee."

A few seconds later, a young man, blond, bronzed, and nude, entered the bedroom carrying a cup. "Here you are, Miss Marwick," he said, smiling.

Abby slipped from between the men, stood, took the coffee and pressed her breasts against Bernie's chest. He responded immediately, caressing her, kissing her face.

"Let's go into the guest room," Abby said, her breathing already rapid.

"Gosh, Miss Marwick, I never met a nympho before." She laughed, groping him. "I bet you could keep an army of men happy."

"God knows I'd do my best," she said, leading him through the living room.

From the television set in the corner came the forecaster's voice: "Hurricane Constance is expected to be downgraded to a tropical storm by late this afternoon as it heads into the cooler water of the south-central Gulf of Mexico. We'll follow the storm's progress closely and keep you informed."

"A hurricane," Abby said thoughtfully. She laughed. "Why not? I guess it's the season for natural disasters. Last night I felt the earth tremble for hours."

"We had an earthquake?" Bernie asked, eyes wide. Abby patted his butt.

"Don't try to think, Bernie," she said. "It spoils the mood."

———

At noon, Al walked from Randy's garage through the old village toward his home. The natives of the old village, particularly the stooped and elderly, had gathered in the street as was their custom when discussing news. It would happen as though by chance, two people meandering along the dirt lane from opposite directions, stopping to pass the time of day. Almost immediately, a door would open and someone would step out, ostensibly to run an errand. Another and another would come forward until a crowd formed and someone would say softly, "Hear tell a storm's blowin' out there off Mexico." Soon everyone would join in hushed, fevered whispers.

As Al approached, they grew silent. Recognizing him, an old woman called, "Al. Hey, Al, you got a nose for stuff such as this. Is Constance coming our way?"

Al put his arm around the woman's shoulder. "Mother," he said although they were not related, "I don't have an idea right now. But I'm going down to take a look at the water, and on my way back I'll tell you what I think. But don't go putting too much stock in it. Half the time even *I* don't believe me." They laughed softly. Al walked on.

He crossed Bienville and continued along past his house. He thought he smelled sausage. Doyle no doubt was preparing lunch. At the end of the road, across from Randy's and Cookie's house, he climbed the dune, reaching the top breathless.

He saw a calm sea and clear sky. Only in the south, just above the horizon, were there high, cottony cumulus clouds. He studied the waves breaking over the sand. They were little more than ripples.

The tide was just beginning to come in. Yet, these tiny waves were already breaking above the high tide line. Al turned and hurried down the dune.

"I don't like it," he told Doyle while they ate the Cajun sausages. "With that storm hundreds of miles out, we're already getting some surge. Tonight, we're putting everything in boxes and tying them up on the rafters. We'll get flooded out here sure as hell, but at least the important stuff'll stay dry."

"You can't tell this soon," Doyle said shaking his head.

"No, not for sure, but I got a feeling."

"I guess the spirits are talking to you, eh, Al? Or you been hittin' the hooch again?"

"Not the hooch, no. As far as the spirits—I'm not smart enough to know about that."

———

Norman Whitney sat on the stern deck of the *Alicia B.* in the shade of a canvas tarp, his feet propped up on the built-in bench and his laptop on his thighs. His fingers moved rapidly over the keys, his brow knit in concentration, when a light breeze ruffled his hair. He looked up, gazed around and smiled. This had been his dream, and he'd almost achieved it.

"That should do it," Randy Manning said, stepping out from beneath the hull of the *Alicia B.* The skeletons of junked cars and decrepit boats surrounded him. "I put eight layers of fiberglass on that sucker. It would be great if the rest of the hull was as tough as that patch."

"I appreciate it, Randy—everything you've done."

"It was just a hairline crack from the forklift. That's all it takes." Fortunately, the boat hadn't actually sunk. The water level had risen only halfway up the engine block before the men got the pumps working. When the bilge was dry, they floated the *Alicia B.* onto the borrowed trailer and, well past midnight, towed it back to the yard. There, they'd opened the hatch, portholes, and drain cocks to give the boat a good airing out. Finally, Norman checked back in at the motel, showered and collapsed on the bed without having eaten dinner.

I'll do a diet book next, he'd thought as sleep overtook him. It'll be tree words long: Buy a boat.

The next morning, Norman met Randy at Milt's Diner.

"You look terrible," Norman told him cheerfully.

"So do you," Randy growled, "and I got a better excuse. I ain't been home all night. After we got your boat to the garage, I ran out to the west end. Some woman's air conditioner was acting up. She needed cooling off."

"Couldn't you go home after that?"

"It took a couple hours. Then I got to working on a car. Never seems to be enough time, especially now with Don gone." Randy paused. Norman saw in his eyes both exhaustion and fire.

"You know," Randy said as though sharing a secret, "I can go days without sleep. Being there in the garage, in the quiet—all over this island people asleep and I'm awake. I walk out there in the yard, look up at the sky. Millions of stars, just *millions*. It's like they're all there just for me, 'cause everybody else is sleeping and I'm awake. Damn, it's awesome!"

"The lure of the forbidden," Norman said.

Randy frowned. "What's that mean?"

Norman shrugged. "Nothing. One of my many boring theories. All good people are expected to be asleep—but you're not. 'Evil' is its own reward. Mischief Night, the night before Halloween, we'd ring doorbells and run like hell. Such fun—because it was forbidden! How many people commit robberies, even murder, just for the thrill of doing what's forbidden? Take sex. I suspect we owe some heavy duty gratitude to the religious folks who keep telling us how sinful sex is. If it weren't so naughty it wouldn't be half the fun."

That was one of the points Norman wanted to make in *A Philosophy of Sex*, but another point was even more important. In fact, it would be the heart of the book. It was not original with him; many others had said the same, most memorably Walt Whitman. After describing the body's wonders, he concluded:

O I say, these are not the parts and poems of the
Body only, but of the Soul,
O I say now these are the Soul!

He was in the mood to begin writing immediately, aboard his boat, surrounded by hulking wrecks of cars. From his perch he could still see gliding gulls above the sound and feel its breeze. He lowered his fingers to the laptop's keyboard, and allowed the words to flow.

"We are not bodies and spirits," he wrote. "We are *bodyspirits*. To say the flesh is evil is absurd, for the flesh is the soul and the soul is the flesh. To condemn the flesh is sacrilege, a blasphemy older than Augustine or St. Paul or Plato—perhaps older than Zoroaster. And it is rooted in the terror of death."

Death leads to the body's disintegration. "From dust we come; to dust we shall return." But the human animal has the unique quality—the unique curse—of self-awareness. Few of us can endure the knowledge of eternal extinction. Somehow some part of us must survive death; so we gave ourselves a sacred soul, and scorned our profane, shamefully sex-driven, soon-to-be rotting bodies. That schism is as untenable as it is phony.

At one-thirty that afternoon, Jessica sat in a wooden lounge chair in the shade of a water oak in front of her motel room. She'd been reading a gothic romance paperback, but her mind wandered to doctors, hospitals, tests. Depressed, she closed her eyes and slept.

She felt something crawling on her upper arm. Yelping, she slapped at it even before opening her eyes.

Norman laughed. He held a long pine needle between his fingers. "I'm sorry," he said. "I was trying to awaken you gently."

"I thought you were a spider," Jessica pouted. Then she brightened. "I bet you had a wonderful night on the water. Did the ripples rock you to sleep?"

"The boat sank."

"No!"

"Well, not exactly, but it did take on water. I think I'd hate my life if I had the energy. No, I don't mean that. As a matter of fact, everything's fine now. This morning Randy patched the hole with fiberglass. And I hope life will get downright wonderful this evening, when I pick you up for dinner in my yacht. Unfortunately, it's still in Randy's yard until early tomorrow morning, when we tie it up in a slip by the Pelican Pub."

Jessica leaned back in the lounge chair. Above her, oak leaves shimmered in a breeze off the Gulf. Sunlight and shadows dappled her face. She glanced at Norman.

"I wonder if I should get my husband's permission first. Do you happen to know the protocol in situations like this?"

"Where is he?"

"At home—in Mobile. I had to be alone, do some heavy thinking." She smiled sheepishly. "I didn't even tell him where I was going. If I had, he'd have raced to the yacht club and been down here a couple of hours after hearing about the bridge."

"Which would be a wise thing for him to do."

Jessica looked up at Norman. "I don't want to leave the island now," she said. "Maybe tomorrow, or the next day, but not yet."

"You'll let him go on worrying about you?"

Jessica took a deep breath. "No, I'll call. I'll phone his private line this afternoon and leave a message that I'm fine, and I'll be home soon. That's all."

She stood and walked past Norman toward her motel room door. Turning, she said, "Dinner with a distinguished professor—I wonder what the neighbors will say."

"We won't have any neighbors. The boat's in Randy's junkyard."

She turned to face him, smiling. "We're celebrating the launch of a boat that's in a junkyard!" She laughed. "What time?"

"I'll pick you up about seven?"

"I'm looking forward to it."

———

Cookie's shift at Milt's Diner ended at three that afternoon, and, soon after, she took off her apron, hung it on the wall hook, kissed Milt on his forehead, and started for the back door.

"I hope you'll get your smile back by tomorrow," the man called after her. Cookie turned back to him and forced a grin.

"Not that one," Milt said. "The real one my customers like so much." Cookie nodded, turned quickly, and left.

She found Randy in the parking lot, sitting on the hood of her red Cadillac. The two gazed into each other's eyes in silence. Finally Cookie turned away.

"I want to talk to you," Randy said. When she heard the pleading in his voice, she faced him.

"Yes, I want talk, too."

"Will you walk with me?"

She meandered west along the boulevard, Randy following. When they reached the lane, they turned and continued toward Heron Bayou and the ramp where Norman's boat had been.

"I don't want you to be unhappy, Cookie," Randy said. "And I sure don't want to be the one making you that way."

Cookie shook her head. She lifted her face to the sky and opened her mouth to breathe deeply. "But I *am* unhappy, Randy. And it *is* you make me feel this way."

"I know. I know, damn it." He threw up his hands in exasperation.

"You don't come home all night last night. Why? You hate me?"

"Oh, no." He stopped, took her in his arms, pulled her against him. "Oh, no, Cookie. I love you."

She pushed him away. "Then why you go to other women?" she shouted. "Why you break my heart? Am I not good wife? I give you all sex you want, every way you want, any time. Cook your food, clean your house, wash your clothes, take care of every need like I was trained? And yet you need other women?" Rubbing her face with the back of her hands, she turned quickly and ran to the water's edge.

Randy followed. He reached for her, then dropped his hands helplessly. "Cookie," he said, "I wish I could explain. I'm not gonna make any excuses. I'm not gonna lie to you. I'm just so damned miserable. I'm bored—oh, not with you and our life together—but that, too, I guess. You know me. I could never stay in one place very long. Soon as I got a job and learned how to do it, it was time to move. I go crazy in that garage all day—I can't stand it. I can't stay there. It's..." He ran both hands through his hair, lifting it out like a lion's mane.

He turned and walked away from her shaking his head. "I just—I don't know how to explain what's wrong. It's like I'm addicted to—to life, doing something important, something that counts, that people will remember me for."

Cookie turned on him. "Will they remember you in bed?"

"What do *you* think?" Randy demanded. "Will *you*?"

Cookie turned away.

"Look, I'm sorry. Let me tell you something. The other day when that bridge went down, and all them government people, the state police, the civil defense, all of them out there, and I was the one actually doing it, getting things done, I felt so pumped. I was really a hundred percent alive. And then the next morning I'm back in the garage working on some damned gear linkage. Can you imagine me thirty years from now sitting on some porch somewhere. 'Randy Manning. Randy Manning? Who the hell's Randy Manning? Oh, yeah. Ain't he the guy ran a garage once over there on DeSoto Avenue? Never did have much business sense. I hear his wife's still waiting tables at Milt's Diner or the poor bastard would be starving to death.'"

"Poor Randy," Cookie said, her voice laden with sorrow. She walked to him and rested the palm of her hand against his face. "All I ever want was you be happy. I try and try, but I don't know how."

"It's not your fault. It's me."

"I hold you down. I make a cage for you, a prison."

Randy started to speak, but she put her fingers to his lips. "What happens? I think so much of Randy I forget his pain." She dropped her hands to her sides and straightened her shoulders. "Somebody say to me, 'Cookie, you are only one can make you happy.' I..." She lowered her gaze and, avoiding Randy's eyes, said, "I want us get divorce."

"Oh, Cookie," Randy whispered, bringing his arm across his forehead. He shook his head. "Don't do this, please."

They were silent. It was that time of the afternoon when the heat and humidity settled on the island and there was neither breeze nor movement. The animals were still, and the birds. Only the buzz of a fly broke the silence.

Finally, Randy said, "If that's really what you want, if that's what I have to do to make you happy..." His voice cracked. He cleared his throat. "I won't try to stop you if you want to divorce me. But in the meantime, I'm going to try like hell to treat you right."

Cookie walked past him toward the boulevard, her arms folded. When he joined her, she said, "I think we should not live together. Want me to move out?"

"The house is yours. I gave it to you, remember? If that's what you want, I'll move into the garage tonight."

Inexplicably to Randy, Cookie burst into tears and ran from him.

CHAPTER XI

At seven that evening, Norman drove to the motel to pick up Jessica. She answered the door in a light beige jumpsuit, her hair tumbling in waves over her shoulders. He noticed the gem-like green of her eyes, the crimson lipstick, gold teardrop earrings.

"You're beautiful," he said, taking her arm.

"I'm over-dressed," she said, noting his shorts, tennis shoes and T-shirt. "I thought the occasion called for it. A girl doesn't get invited to dinner in a junkyard every day."

He chuckled. "You're perfect."

"Thank you!" she said. "I haven't felt beautiful in a long time. You'll make me very self-satisfied if you're not careful."

They drove from the motel through the gates of Randy's garage, wound around the mounds of tires, rusting engines, cars and boats, and stopped at the *Alicia B.*

"With the bridge out, I wasn't able to get the elevator installed yet," Norman said. "I did run an extension cord from the garage, though, and scraped up a ladder."

Jessica laughed. "I can handle a ladder just fine. I've always been something of a tomboy." Norman climbed up first, and took her hand as Jessica stepped over the gunwale. He led her to one of the cushioned holding tanks in the cockpit.

"Make yourself comfortable. I'll put on some music and bring us champagne."

It really is lovely, she thought when he left. Across the street and west of the Pelican Pub stretched the Mississippi Sound, its placid surface reflecting the blue-purple of the sky, its myriad stars.

At the horizon, a blazing blood-red and purple streak shaded to blue.

From the cabin below, she heard Tchaikovsky's "Swan Lake." A moment later, Norman placed two inexpensive brown coffee cups and an ice bucket holding champagne. He filled the cups.

"They were out of champagne glasses at the general store," he said, tapping his mug to hers. She smiled and sipped. The bubbles tickled her nose.

Turning to the horizon, she said, "You're very kind to go to this trouble. It's so lovely here."

They were silent for a while, sipping champagne and watching the sun dip lower until only a stiletto blade of brilliance streaked across the water.

"It's not all it's cracked up to be," Norman said. "The fishing's lousy."

Jessica laughed. After a moment, she said, "You seem so at ease… at peace with yourself."

Norman rose to refill her champagne glass.

"I guess I follow Solomon's philosophy: 'Eat, drink, and be merry, for tomorrow we die.'"

"So nothing matters in the end?" Jessica asked softly. "Rather depressing."

"In fact, *everything* matters, but pleasure—in its broadest sense—matters most of all. We exist to seek and find pleasure. In the satisfaction of helping others. Watching children play, hearing them laugh. In the beauty of nature, listening to great music, art.

"But tonight," he continued, "we seek pleasure in eating, drinking, and being merry. Please follow me."

He stood, took her hand, led her through the pilot house and down the steps to the small galley, where he lit two citronella candles to keep the mosquitoes at bay. They sat at a tiny table he'd set with mismatched dishes, forks, and spoons, and a shared knife. A tall red candle flickered from a glass holder painted with the words, "Alabama's Gulf Coast." Neatly folded across the plates were two napkins matching the color of the candles and with the same welcoming words.

Turning from the table, Norman stooped beneath the stove to the tiny refrigerator and retrieved two small bowls brimming with avocado and grapefruit slices on a bed of spinach. He placed the salads on the table along with a jar of poppy seed dressing.

"How lovely," Jessica said as Norman slid into the seat across from her. "Where on earth did you find grapefruit and avocados?"

"From the Isle Dauphine restaurant. Same with the champagne, shrimp, asparagus, and cognac for later. With the bridge out, they're not expecting much business. The rare china and silver were tougher. I found them on the floor of the john in Manning's garage. No need for concern—I scrubbed and scalded them to death. More champagne?"

Jessica smiled. Her eyes reflected the flicker of the candle. "Thank you," she whispered.

"We'll eat, and drink—and later, if you like, we'll drive to the beach and be merry watching the waves roll in."

———

The second floor of the Pelican Pub trembled with the beat of sixties rock, and the crowd's energy. Every table and every seat at the bar was occupied. Scores more gathered on the deck below, where the crab and shrimp boiled and Lou Parrish shucked oysters. Children dodged tables as they raced around the pub and up and down the stairs between the lounge and the ground floor restaurant.

Abby Marwick took an oyster from Lou and sucked it seductively. "What have you done with my dance floor?" she asked, pouting.

"This is family night, Abby," Lou answered, pecking her on the cheek.

"Wednesday was always Wet T-Shirt Night. I looked forward to it."

"You think I didn't?" Lou laughed. "That was before London Bridge came falling down. But I've got to cater to the people still here, and that means families."

"I'm still here."

Lou patted her butt and bent to whisper in her ear, "I promise you the best catering you ever had, one on one, if you're here at closing time." Abby laughed and spun away.

In the center of the dance floor, Al Reed sat at a large round table cluttered with crab and oyster shells, discarded heads and tails of shrimp, bags of potato chips, pitchers of beer, and, in front of Al, three cans of 7-Up. Ruth and Don sat beside him. Randy, who neither ate nor drank, but stopped in to show support, stood nearby.

Zechariah Ledbetter, from the general store, had come by on his way back to the old village because, he said, he needed a beer to keep his circulation going. Yet, he searched the crowded room intensely, and when he found Al, he moved directly to his table, dragging an empty chair with him.

"I was just telling Randy here, Zechariah," Al said, "this is the dumbest name for a place I ever heard in my life. The Pelican Pub—bah."

"Why so, Al?"

"Did you ever see pelican on the menu even once?"

"Can't say as I have."

"Did you ever sell pelican, fresh or frozen, in your store? See it on the menu at Milt's or the Isle Dauphine? No, you haven't, and you know why? It's 'cause people don't eat pelicans. And you don't need a Pelican Pub 'cause pelicans don't *go* to pubs!"

"You're right, Al," said Zach. "Hey Lou," he yelled. Lou Parrish looked up. "Why'd you ever name this place the Pelican Pub?"

Lou shrugged. "I liked the way it sounded," he shouted. "It's called alliteration."

"Well, I wasn't going to let that bastard husband of mine kill Don," Ruth Knebles said. "So I call the old coot this afternoon and I tell him, I say, 'Look, I know you gotta save face—although God knows if I had a face ugly as yours I'd give it away in a snap. I been thinking it over and I'm gonna give you a break. We'll both come out of it better off—and I'll be alive, which is a benefit. I'll settle for half a million, the condo, and the Caddy, and sign off on everything else. You'll still have fifteen million bucks. You'll save the cost of the hit man. You don't have to risk getting zapped for murder. And you won't have to lay awake nights with your conscience torturing you because you killed your sweet old wife. Either go with the deal or take your best shot, you bastard.'"

Everyone laughed.

"So what did he say?" Randy asked.

"Say? For five minutes he just laughed! Then he says, 'You know, you still got it, baby. Nobody—I mean *nobody* but you—would dare talk to me like that. You still got the biggest balls in the south. Okay, you got your half mil. Now, good riddance to you.' And he slams the phone down."

"So you're free?" Don asked, his eyes wide. He took her hand in his.

"Free as a bird," she said. Of course, soon as I get the money and the signed deed, I'm going to the feds. Nobody's selling drugs to kids if I can help it."

Old Zach cleared his throat. "So, ah, Al."

"What is it, Zechariah?"

"They say the storm, that there Constance, it's headed for Texas and won't amount to much."

"Yeah, that's what they say, Zechariah."

"I guess they might be right. What with all them satellites and such."

"Well, they usually are. They get the radar, and fly right through the storm—how they live to tell it I'll never know. Crazy is what it is."

"It's crazy is what it is," old Zach repeated, slapping the table. He took a sip of beer from the pitcher. "All they'd have to do is ask somebody with experience, somebody like you, for instance, where it's gonna make landfall."

"Well, now," Al said, leaning back with a can of 7-Up in his hand. "If they *was* to ask me, which they won't, I think I'd have to tell them this ain't one of them times they're gonna be right."

Old Zach leaned forward, his eyes widening in secretive glee.

"No, there's high pressure moving in all along that line from Panama to northern Mexico. It's drifting northeast, a solid wall of heavy air running north to south. Probably off Texas by now. That Constance'll never get through it."

Zechariah slapped the table again. "That's just what I been sayin'. It ain't going to Texas. No it ain't."

"It *can't.* Gonna run along that ridge of high pressure north, come in somewheres east of Texas, maybe Mississippi."

"*Sure* it is!"

"That's where all the hot and humid air and water is, just like in '69."

"Frederic?" someone asked.

"No, no," Al chuckled, waving the suggestion away. "That was Camille in '69. Worst storm ever to hit the Gulf Coast. Oh, sure, Frederic was worse here on the island, no two ways about it. The wind alone tore whole sections out of that wooden bridge used to be there, tossed 'em all over hell. They clocked Frederic's winds at a hundred and thirty-five miles an hour—that was the constant wind, not the gusts. You know how fast that is? Winds that fast can lift a full-grown man off his feet, make him think he's flying like a bird. That wind snapped pines like they was toothpicks, tossed 'em a quarter mile."

"But this one don't put you in mind of Frederic?" Zach and Al seemed to be having a private conversation while the others eavesdropped.

"Nah. Frederic, if you remember, was a hurricane out in the Atlantic long before it got to the Caribbean. Then the thing just dropped dead over Cuba. Remember? It wasn't even a storm no more, just—I guess they call it a disturbance. Then it hit the Gulf waters and bang, back full force.

"Curious thing, that Frederic—it was the wind did most of the damage. Actually, it hit the bay and sound from the north, blew the waters out toward the Gulf, not in, like most storms. You

112

could've walked across Mobile Bay, they tell me, except for the ship channel.

"People here thought they was safer building along the sound than out on the Gulf, but that storm sure fooled 'em. Wind came howling out of the north, ripped them houses apart like they was made of cardboard."

"So you think it's more like Camille in '69?" Zach asked.

"God, I hope not!" Al said, shaking his head. "We dodged a bullet with that one. People forget. Maybe it's just as well. Them winds were record breakers—two hundred miles an hour. Slammed twenty-foot-high waves into Gulfport, Biloxi. We got by with winds in the seventies, maybe twelve feet of water across the island. Everybody evacuated except old cranks like you, Zechariah. You guys stayed over there in the village, and damned if you didn't make it."

Those at the table laughed. Zach took another swig of beer from the pitcher and allowed himself the trace of a smile.

"So, which one's this remind you of?" Ruth asked.

"Well, that's just the point," Al said. "It don't remind me of none of 'em. Them storms were all in August, September—not July. They started out off the African coast. This one here, this Constance, she was born right down there in the Caribbean. Such storms mostly go up the east coast. Maybe across Florida. We ain't never had a severe storm got born in the Caribbean. Not until now."

"But she's trackin' the same as an Atlantic storm—that your point?" old Zach asked.

"That's it exactly. That, and just a feeling."

Abby Marwick and her friends meandered over to listen to the conversation. One of them said, "I'm not worried. Dauphin Island has always been here and always will be."

"Not true," Al said, standing. "Been here only about six thousand years, when some big storm came by and tore a pass between here and the mainland, right through the swamp, dug out the Sound. Before that it was part of the continent. And you know, it's been changing shape every day since then, a little more sand here, a little less there."

Abby Marwick laughed harshly. "Everything changes, and everything stays the same—that's what I think."

Al nodded, smiling. "That's as good a way to look at it as any, if you ask me. True of people, true of islands." He took his can of 7-Up and, waving, left the table.

———

Walking home that night, he realized he hadn't even mentioned Eleana, the 1985 storm that bashed the entire Gulf coast from Panama City to Biloxi with 122-mile-an-hour winds and a storm surge that swept over virtually all of Dauphin Island, burying asphalt under tons of sand. And all those in-between storms, the ones without names, the constant barrage of weather. It would have been like describing God, exhausting and futile, and he wasn't up to it. As sure as he knew the spirits in the night, he knew that, like his own existence, the island was ephemeral and eternal. Someday a storm would come that would obliterate it from the earth, and then, centuries or millennia later, another storm would recreate it, and so it would go.

———

Betsy Smith's last thoughts before sleeping were of Abby Marwick. The love she felt for Abby was deeper, she admitted without guilt, than even her feelings for Bill. No, not deeper really, but more expansive, enduring. It was similar to the way she loved her children, tolerant, uncritical. Even when they were kids, Abby always made her laugh, always did outrageous things. To be in her presence made Betsy feel alive. Only recently, as Abby's life seemed to be falling apart, did she bring Betsy sorrow.

CHAPTER XII

In the *Alicia B.*, Norman and Jessica were just finishing the shrimp scampi.

"What's the wonderful seasoning?" Jessica asked.

"Must be the basil," Norman said. "It's a simple recipe—garlic, salt, and basil in melted butter. You have to get the pan hot so the shrimp cook quickly—a couple of minutes, no more."

"It's great."

"The champagne—that's the *real* secret. Drink enough of it and anything tastes great." He emptied the bottle into both cups.

Later, he put the dishes in the sink, went to the refrigerator and brought out two small cups of raspberries smothered in whipped cream. Placing them on the table, he asked, "Coffee or tea?"

"Tea, thanks."

Lemon or cream?"

"Lemon, and half a spoon of sugar."

While the water heated, Norman sat across from Jessica. He leaned toward her, studied her face.

"My students and colleagues think I'm an egghead intellectual," he said, smiling. "I have a confession to make."

"About what?"

"Well, I adhere to some seriously irrational ideas. For example, I've been known to pray. What's the harm in it? And it makes me feel good."

Jessica laughed. "Last I heard, they can't fire you for that."

"That's not all. I also believe in fate. I think it was fate that brought us both to the same motel, had us leave our rooms at the same time. What do you think?"

Jessica lifted a spoonful of raspberries to her mouth.

"Mmm! Perfect. Just enough sweetness in the cream. You could be a chef."

"And ruin a delightful hobby? Never."

Jessica lowered the spoon. She sighed, stared up at the ceiling.

All right," she said softly, and looked into Norman's eyes. "Maybe I can't think this through by myself. Maybe I need a counselor or priest or something—what do you charge? Maybe fate did bring us together, except I don't believe in fate.

"My mother died of breast cancer. I've never had children. I take—I should say *did* take—birth control pills—female hormones. Those are three major risk factors. I insisted on a biopsy immediately. It wasn't only breast cancer but a somewhat aggressive form. It might already have metastasized to other organs. They were talking chemo and radiation. I told them I wanted surgery immediately. I go under the knife (don't you just hate that expression?) next Monday at six a.m. I'm not particularly optimistic."

His lips pressed together, Norman nodded slightly.

The teakettle whistled. A moment later Norman set two cups of tea, slices of lemon and a small bottle of sugar on the table.

"Help yourself," he said. Leaning back after sipping the tea, he said, "I think you made the right decision. Time is of the essence."

"I hope so." Norman saw the dampness in her eyes. "I'm frightened," she whispered. He took her hand.

117

"Of course you are. I'd be astonished if you weren't. In fact, I'm frightened *for* you. But we can both do something to help ourselves. We can find a place of peace inside ourselves, somewhere as serene as the Sound out there tonight, as tranquil as the stars—find that place and retire to it whenever fear threatens us. I know it's possible, Jessica. I've done it. We'll do it together, shall we?"

Tears ran down Jessica's cheeks. She nodded, smiled. "Let's just hope that storm—Constance—doesn't come this way," she said, "or I might miss my date with the butcher." They laughed.

"Speaking of the weather..." Norman reached behind him and placed a small battery-powered weather radio on the table.

"...tropical storm became a hurricane at 5:46 this evening, and is now headed due north. She is still expected to make landfall between Corpus Christi and Galveston, Texas, but Constance remains unpredictable, and may come in west of New Orleans, Louisiana. At present it appears she will make landfall in the early hours of Friday morning, but the National Weather Service stresses it is too soon to make any absolute predictions.

"Constance is now producing sustained winds of one hundred twenty miles an hour, with gusts up to one hundred forty miles an hour. The city of New Orleans is particularly susceptible to severe flood damage. Much of it is situated fourteen feet below sea level. Levees theoretically protect the city from the higher water of Lake Ponchartrain, but some have questioned the adequacy of these levies, warning that any severe surge could inflict incalculable destruction to life and property in the city."

Norman shut off the radio.

"You know, Jessica said, "I haven't had a pleasant evening since I came to this island—until now. This was worth waiting for."

She smiled. "I must say, I feel as though this has been a breakthough. I came here to think, but I've been avoiding it. Until now." She reached across the table.

For a long while they sat holding hands, watching the candlelight dance in each other's eyes.

Jessica cleared her throat. "How's the book coming?" she asked.

"What? Oh, I worked on it all afternoon. I don't know about the writing, but at least what it says is important."

"What's that?"

"Everywhere you look, people are worshipping...the intellect. What we forget is our intellects are nothing more than tools to preserve the body, which existed thousands of years before human intellect as we know it today. And the truths of the body were the primary truths, and still are— love, rage, passion, the senses. Those are the ultimate truths."

Jessica laughed. "You're not suggesting we all go back to wearing loincloths and living in caves?"

Norman smiled. "No on both counts. Caves are limiting in terms of creature comforts and views, and loincloths wouldn't be necessary in a body-positive society."

"We should all go naked?"

"Why not? Body shame isn't natural. No child wants to be dressed. Have you ever swum nude?"

Jessica blushed. She cleared her throat. "We had a mud hole on the farm. I stopped when I began...when I became a teenager." She paused. "I remember it was fun."

They searched each other's eyes in silence. Finally, Jessica's gaze faltered.

"Wow," she said. "It must be the champagne."

"And we haven't even had the cognac yet."

"Is it warm in here, or is it just me?"

"I tell you what—there's a beautiful breeze down at the beach this time of night. Let's drive down. We can have a nightcap there, and then I'll drop you off at the motel."

Jessica nodded in agreement. She felt delightfully muddleheaded. "A wonderful end to a glorious evening," she said. "Just make sure I don't fall off the ladder on my way down."

Norman descended first and reached up to hold Jessica around the waist. He felt her body tremble at his touch.

"You know," he said in an attempt to put her at ease, to distract her, "this afternoon, the strangest irony occurred to me. I'll be spending two hundred fifty, maybe three hundred pages building an argument to give the truths of the body their rightful position of superiority to the truths of the intellect. And my entire argument is built on *intellectual* truth!" They both laughed.

———

At dusk, Cookie telephoned Al's house and spoke with Doyle. "I make some good cookies, chocolate chip, for you and Al," she said. "You want them, I bring them to you on dune, half hour. Yes?"

"Sure," Doyle answered. "Sure!"

They met as night settled softly over the water. The sky was clear, and a multitude of stars punctured the darkness. They sat close, Doyle gulping a tuna salad sandwich Cookie had brought him.

Finally, Cookie said, "They still look for you. The cops come to Milt's this afternoon, asking."

"Anybody tell them anything?"

"No, no. See no evil, hear no evil, speak no evil." They laughed. "What you gonna do, Doyle?"

"I don't know. Turn myself in, I guess. What else *can* I do?" In the darkness Cookie shook her head.

"You make mistake. We all make mistake."

"Yeah, but mine cost a hell of a lot of money. I almost killed some people."

"But you didn't."

Doyle took a deep breath and let it out slowly. "I was such a fool, Cookie, running eighteen hours—regulations say twelve's the limit. Lousy equipment—the lines should have been replaced. I was cutting corners everywhere to compete with the big boys. Something had to happen sooner or later."

He paused, breathing deeply, dropping his head back to stare at the stars. "I knew I shouldn't have gone out there drunk," he whispered. "I *knew* it, but I went ahead and did it."

Cookie thought she heard him sob. She moved behind him and rested her hands on his shoulders. Gently she kneaded the muscles. They were like steel.

"Relax, Doyle," she whispered. "That better."

Far down the beach, they saw the silhouettes of a man and woman walking toward the water. They stopped, sat in the sand, illuminated against a phosphorescent sea. A few moments later, Doyle and Cookie watched as they undressed, throwing their clothes farther up on the sand. Holding hands, they turned toward the water. The man ran ahead, diving into the waves. Slowly, the woman followed.

"Long time ago," Cookie said, her voice quivering, "Randy and I do that. We do that every night, right down there." She pointed to the waves.

Doyle took her hand. "I wouldn't have the nerve," he said. "I'm too shy."

He saw in the moonlight that she smiled. "You silly, Doyle," she said. "Silly American. In Korea, fathers, mothers, children bathe naked, swim naked together. No big deal."

"Yeah, that's like it should be. No big deal. Trouble is, I was born and raised here, and for some reason we make it a big deal. And I'm still too shy."

She squeezed his hand. For the first time that day, Doyle smiled.

———

The waist-high waves drained the night's sultry heat from their bodies. Jessica lowered herself into the coolness. Submerged, she spread her knees and kicked like a frog, luxuriating in the water's caress. It touched her everywhere, lightly, embracing.

She stood, laughing.

"I'm lighthearted. No—light*headed*. The world's spinning."

"That's true," Norman said. She couldn't see him.

"I know, but I mean—"

"I know what you mean." He stood just behind her, the water rippling against his knees. She studied his body unabashedly.

"With the moonlight on you like that, you look like you're made of marble," she said. "Like a Roman statue."

"You're beautiful, Jessica," he told her.

"You're not bad yourself," she said, tapping him on the shoulder. "You're *it*!" Laughing, she spun away and dove into the waves.

Norman followed, searching futilely. Suddenly she stood twenty feet from him. With a powerful leap, he streaked toward her, but again she vanished. She came to the surface near the shore. This time he approached beneath the surface. Standing, he gently caressed her shoulder. She shrieked in surprise.

"You're it," he said softly.

"It," she gasped, touching his cheek.

He put his hand behind her head and softly kissed her. "It."

She embraced him, kissed him, still gasping.

"I think I need to rest," she said.

———

At three-thirty that morning, the island was still. The Pelican Pub had been closed for an hour, and Randy's garage was smothered in darkness. Randy himself lay on the tiny cot, a sheen of sweat covering him. He hadn't been able to sleep, thinking of Cookie and their life.

He heard a car approach and stop. The engine went dead. A door opened and closed, followed by footsteps in the yard. Quickly, silently, Randy picked up the pipe he always kept beside the cot. He moved quickly in bare feet between the shadows to the one door that had no lock, and stood behind it, waiting.

The doorknob turned. Randy raised the pipe in both hands.

"Randy, baby, it's your l'le Abby here for a tune-up." Randy lowered his arms.

"I could have knocked your brains out," he said. "What are you doing here so late?"

"I'm bored. I'm drunk, and I'm still bored."

Randy walked back to the living quarters and turned on a lamp.

"Come on, I'll make some coffee."

"I don't want coffee. I want you." She took his hand and led him toward the cot.

"Don't do this," Randy said. "The sheet's all sweaty. You don't want me. I haven't had a shower in a day and a half and I'm greasy."

"Don't tell me what I want, Randy. I'm a big girl now."

"I don't want to do this, Abby," he said emphatically. But his flesh responded to her caresses. He took her face in his hands, kissing her lips. Sitting on the cot, he pulled her down beside him.

"Why don't you just go to sleep?"

She began caressing his chest and abdomen. "Will you undress me and put me to bed?"

"Yes, Abby, I will."

He knelt before her, unbuttoned her blouse, slipped it over her shoulders along with the bra. She lay back on the pillow, her eyes closed, reached up, put her hand on Randy's neck, and pulled his face to her breasts.

"Oh, Abby," he whispered. "I don't want to do this. I really don't." Yet, he stretched his body over hers.

THURSDAY

CHAPTER XIII

A storm's destiny is written in caprice. Its birth is an accident of winds and temperatures, its progress dictated by upper level steering currents. In the darkness of predawn that Thursday, Constance churned two hundred miles of Gulf waters with gale force winds. The wall of fury surrounding its calm eye beat waves to thirty-foot heights, and reached gusts of one hundred twenty miles an hour.

Yet, from a human perspective, all that energy and display signified nothing. Not a single ship foundered in her raging anger. Caught in the tug of the easterlies, her future seemed predictable. She would stall out well off the coast of Cuba and die there in cool water, an insignificant footnote in meteorology data books.

The night before, a ridge of high pressure had formed due west of the hurricane, as Al had predicted. It, too, had its accidents of birth—cool air blowing off the Andes, a glitch in the southern jet stream, high pressure in the southwestern quadrant of the Gulf of Mexico. Heavy, and towering well into the troposphere, that immovable, impenetrable bumper forced the easterlies northward. Constance came to a standstill. But an upper level low at latitude 28° N, longitude 92° W, created a trough of warm, moist air. Finally, that Thursday morning, the storm began moving along that trough toward the northeast. By sunrise, it was three hundred thirty miles south-southwest of New Orleans and traveling at fourteen miles an hour.

On the island, the barometric pressure had already begun to drop. From the marshes, the egrets had flown across the sound to the mainland. The pelicans had abandoned their roosts along the rails of the damaged bridge and pilings of the docks. The sea gulls and sandpipers had fled, too, some beyond Mobile. The tiny sand crabs had burrowed deep, leaving the beaches empty. All was silent.

When the sun rose, the sky was red and dusty. The waves, driven by a continuous, gentle wind from the southwest, could be heard across the entire island.

At the garage, Randy held Abby tightly in his arms while she sobbed.

"That was great, Randy," she said. "Why is it the only time I feel whole is when I'm in bed with some guy?"

Randy caressed her hair, slid his hand over her shoulder and down her back.

"You got everything, Abby—looks, money, youth," he said. "Why the hell can't you be happy?"

"If I knew that—at least I'd know something, huh? I told you last night, we're two sick dudes, you and me. There's no percentage in it, no future. But we're here just the same, aren't we?"

Suddenly Randy stood, put on his briefs and jeans, pushed a button on the coffee machine, and turned on a radio.

"Come on, let's cuddle," Abby pouted.

"...four-thirty a.m., turned sharply north-northeast," the radio blared, "and is now moving at fifteen miles an hour toward the coast of Louisiana. Right now, the entire Gulf Coast from eastern Texas to the Florida panhandle is under a hurricane watch. Constance is expected to either stall and break up or make landfall within the next twenty-four hours. According to the National Hurricane Center in Coral Gables, Florida, the path of the storm is unpredictable at this point, but the Center has issued a storm advisory from New Orleans east to Pensacola, Florida. If you are in that area, especially if you live along the coast or near bodies of water, you should prepare to evacuate if necessary."

Randy shut off the radio.

"Come on, Abby, let's get you up and packing."

"Packing? Where am I going?"

"Mobile, I guess. We gotta get the island evacuated. We could be in for a hell of a situation here."

"You think I'm going off and leaving my house and car here?" she said. "Besides, what's to do in Mobile?"

"What's to do here?" Randy asked.

"You."

Randy studied her face, her eyes soft, imploring.

"If that storm hits, people are gonna die," he said, touching her cheek with his fingers.

"I'm not going," she said firmly, turning away. Then she confronted him. "Look, Randy, I've got the best-built house on this whole damned island—pre-stressed, steel-reinforced concrete. I push a button and steel shutters protect every door and window. Generators keep the refrigerator cold and the oven warm. There's enough booze in the bar to keep me happy for a month. In fact," she said, slipping into her panties, "I just might throw a hurricane party."

Randy pulled her to him, crushing her against him. He caressed her hair and said, "Abby, you're so crazy."

"I know," she answered.

———

Everyone waited. Along the coast and on the island long-time residents nailed the same plywood they'd used for previous storms across doors and windows. Many with private boats had already left, and some vacationers who had driven to the island had taken the ferry back to the mainland. A second barge was brought in and an additional landing ramp constructed at Billy Goat Hole. Two lines of cars, one for the ferry, the other for the barge, stretched along the median and shoulders of the boulevard.

———

Early in the day, the local and national press began arriving on the island. A local NBC affiliate in Mobile had fed a story to the network about a couple of thousand vacationers who were stranded on an island that might be in the path of a hurricane, and the inherent drama spread like a flash fire through the other networks, major newspapers, and news magazines. Helicopters crisscrossed the sky above Dauphin Island. Speedboats arrived with reporters, sound engineers, and cameramen.

Cameras focused on the gently rippling froth along the beach while celebrity newsmen intoned, "Right now the Gulf of Mexico is a kitten, but in just 24 hours it may be a raging beast tearing at the heart of this tiny island."

At Martin's Marina, another reporter played a variation on the theme: While a cameraman panned the boats in their slips and on dry dock, the reporter said, "Things are peaceful and even charming here on Dauphin Island today. But by this time tomorrow, these handsome vessels could be a pile of rubble."

————

The crowd Randy assembled at Milt's Diner included every emergency and fire department volunteer on the island. Shoulder to shoulder, they stood in silence while the TV displayed file footage of previous hurricanes and a meteorologist recited a litany of preparations already underway:

"Richard Barnett, chairman of the Mobile chapter of the American Red Cross, told me local disaster action teams have been placed on standby. The Alabama division office in Birmingham is prepared to dispatch forty disaster specialists and twenty emergency disaster vehicles to Mobile, should Constance change course again and head our way."

Like a sportscaster describing a football play, the meteorologist explained a multicolored chart of the Gulf Coast, a pie-shaped wedge, its point at the hurricane's eye, flaring to Texas, Louisiana, Mississippi, Alabama, and Florida. The tiny counter-clockwise-turning propeller representing the storm seemed insignificant in contrast to the sweeping coastline. The weatherman continued:

"Mobile County Civil Defense Director David Dennis considers this storm, and I quote, 'a very much unknown situation,' and has prompted his agency to assume a state of readiness. Dennis has urged the public, particularly in low-lying areas such as Gulf Shores, Bayou La Batre, and Dauphin Island, to take all precautions and be prepared to evacuate.

"Dauphin Island is of special concern because on Monday a runaway barge destroyed the bridge there. Dennis also advised people to closely monitor through the media the hurricane's progress and follow all evacuation orders and instructions.

"But Director Dennis has asked me to stress that this is merely a hurricane watch at this time. No warnings have been issued. Conditions are such that Constance could change direction—even radically—at any moment. In fact, she could simply fall apart. Evacuation at this time is not necessary."

"Damn," said Al, "they actually mentioned Dauphin Island. They *never* mention this place. It's like we're not even part of the continent."

"Well," said Don Long, "we're not. We're an island."

"But they mentioned us this time," Al said, awe in his voice.

"...in Bayou La Batre said they were sitting tight and listening," continued the meteorologist. "At Eglin Air Force Base, officials put seven hundred mobile home residents on notice that they might be evacuated to two base community buildings by early this evening. Stay tuned to this station for frequent weather updates."

Those who had been tensely silent a moment before now relaxed into a buzz of chatter. Three reporters who had found their way to the diner began asking questions.

"How concerned are you about Constance?"

"It won't amount to nothing," someone answered "They never do when they come out of the southwest like that."

"Reminds me of Eleana," another responded. "She went every which way before she made up her mind where she was coming ashore."

"Well, I hope to God this one goes where she went. Mississippi can have her."

"I think we ought to be taking this thing seriously," Randy said. The crowd around him settled into silence again. Behind the counter, Cookie and Milt Goldberg ceased washing dishes.

"What are you doing to hasten evacuation?" asked a reporter.

Randy was about to speak when the door opened and two officers in the brown and tan uniforms of the Mobile County Sheriff's Department stepped in.

"Gentlemen," the tall one said, nodding. "We're looking for Doyle Donahue."

Al stared into his coffee.

"Me, too," said old Zach Ledbetter. "He's got a tab at my store, owes me thirty-seven dollars and fifty-two cents."

"What's he done?" Randy asked.

"Leaving the scene of an accident. Reckless endangerment, destroying state property, probably piloting under the influence. That's just for starters."

"Who's Doyle Donahue?" a journalist asked.

"Piloted the tug that took the bridge out."

"So," said the other officer, "where is he?"

There were mutterings and heads shaking no.

"Last I seen him was Friday morning, if I'm not mistaken," Milt Goldberg offered. "He was in for breakfast—a big eater, that guy. Said he was headed for New Orleans to pick up a tow."

"He must be here someplace," the tall officer demanded. "That's his tug, isn't it?" The men all nodded. "But nobody's seen him, right?" Again they shook their heads.

The officer grimaced in disgust and turned to leave.

"Say, officer," Randy said, "is the Sheriff's Department doing anything to evacuate the island?"

The officer turned back to face the men, his arms folded over his chest. "We've got a plan in place," he said. "We'll start evacuation as soon as we know for sure which way the storm's heading." When the officers left, the three journalists followed, asking questions about conducting a manhunt during a hurricane evacuation.

"This is what we have to do," Randy said. "Lou, get in touch with the Coast Guard. Get them to commandeer another ferry—use your charm. We've got to get serious about getting people and their cars off the island. Moving fifty or sixty cars every two hours ain't gonna cut it. There's *two thousand* people here.

"Al, get a crew together and clean up the garage. It's not much, but it's the biggest building on the island, and it's well above the high tide line. I don't think we'll have to worry about a surge in the sound. Some of you other guys gather up mattresses, blankets, cans of food, bottled water. You know what we need—you've been through it before."

Several men nodded their assent.

"Don, you and Ruth round up some volunteers. Cover east of LeMoyne, every street, every house. Tell everybody they gotta be off the island by five o'clock tonight. Tell them about Billy Goat Hole. We'll try to get volunteer boaters to join with the Coast Guard out there. A couple thousand people's a hell of a lot to move in a day."

Except for Cookie, Ruth Knebles was the only woman at Milt's Diner. "You got it, boss," she said. "Come on, Don, let's get moving." She grabbed Don's hand and led him to the door. The men laughed.

"I'm gonna need four volunteers to cover the west end house by house. It's gotta be done right—

nobody'll survive out there if we take a dead hit. I want every house evacuated."

"They won't leave, not all of them," Al muttered, staring at the floor. "There's always some ain't got no idea what it's like. Some guy last time said he had to protect his property." He shook his head. "What's a puny human being gonna do in the face of *that*? Never did find his body."

"As fire chief, I'm also head of Civil Defense on this island," Randy said. "Evacuation by five p.m. isn't an option, it's an order. You tell them that!" Immediately, several men raised their hands to volunteer.

"Good, you six get going, and keep in touch. You can reach me by phone, CB, or VHF. I'll be at the garage."

One after another, the men left the diner. Finally, only Milt, Cookie, and Randy stood together in silence. Milt excused himself.

"I gotta nail up the plywood," he said. "I always have plywood. Year in, year out, I store it. I know sooner or later I'll be nailing it up." He slipped out the back door.

Randy stood at the counter. He watched Cookie pick up a dish, wash it, put it into the drying rack. She returned to the sink, stopped, stared into the suds. He moved toward her. When she turned, her eyes focused on his chest, his neck, finally his face.

"Cookie, I've thought about us all night. I think I know how hard it's been. I can even understand why you can't stay with me—*I* sure as hell wouldn't put up with me. I just want to ask you two things. I want you to promise you'll be safe if this lousy storm hits. I want you to get on the ferry first thing this afternoon. Go to the mainland and find a place you'll be safe. I'll give you some money."

"You don't have money."

"I'll borrow some. I want you to do that, Cookie, so I won't worry."

"I won't leave island. I stay here, where I belong." She looked up at her husband, her eyes damp.

"All right, stay then. But come to the garage. Or if not that, then promise me—*promise* me, Cookie, you'll go somewhere safe."

She nodded.

"And the other thing..." Randy swallowed. "Please say you'll forgive me. I can't—I just can't live knowing... You're the only one in the world I love, Cookie." He moved behind the counter and took her in his arms.

"Oh, Randy," she sobbed. "Sure I forgive you. I always forgive you. I love. I just can't stand to hurt."

———

Jessica and Norman sat beside the glass wall of the Isle Dauphine Restaurant and watched the waves roll gently up the shore. The sun still hadn't burned through the dusty haze, and the sky remained a bright, eerie orange-yellow. Jessica locked her hands behind her neck, leaned back, and breathed deeply. She had been feeling almost giddy since Norman had picked her up an hour earlier.

"You know what I discovered last night after dropping you off?" he asked. "With enough champagne you can feel the boat rolling on the waves—even in dry dock."

Jessica smiled.

"You seem content," he said softly.

"I am. I really am—now. Last night I felt a bit guilty—especially when we were in the water."

"I know. I could tell. You were quiet. But you did nothing wrong."

"After you dropped me off I stood at the bathroom mirror and thought—oh, I don't want to sound morbid, because that's not how I felt at all—I thought I might be a few months away from dying. If for just one night I can cast aside the rules, live free listening to the waves, looking up at a sky full of stars, feeling more alive than I ever thought possible.... Life's pretty good, at least for now." She sighed.

He took her hand.

For a while they sipped their coffee, picked at the French toast on their plates, and watched a few children playing along the beach.

"Hard to believe we could be in a hurricane in twenty-four hours," Norman said.

"It's headed for New Orleans, isn't it? That's what they said on the TV news."

"Even so, I'd like you to leave with me this afternoon."

Jessica laughed. "You don't have to ask me twice. One brush with death this week is enough. But..." She turned away, gazing out the window. "I'm sorry it's ending so quickly."

"I am, too, Jessica." He cleared his throat. "Assuming the hurricane's still headed our way, I'll come to your room around four this afternoon and we'll drive to the ferry. I'll drop you off in Mobile wherever you like." He paused, his eyes widening. "It really would be something to stay—assuming we'd survive."

"Why on earth?"

Norman shrugged. "The adventure, the danger. To do *manly* things." Norman pounded his chest with both fists. "Batten down the hatches, tie off the boats, rescue the virgins, that sort of thing. And be with you."

Jessica leaned over and kissed his cheek. "Then let's stay, brave one. If only for the virgins' sake."

"Oh, no, no. I understand the male of the species has this testosterone thing, this need to overcome impossible odds, stand at the edge of the earth and tower over all." He sipped his coffee. "And part of me longs for that, to do it all—like Randy. But the truth is, I'm not the hero type. I'll settle for reading about it in the papers."

CHAPTER XIV

Before noon, the crews dredging the channel and removing debris ceased work. Tugs pushed barges to the safety of Fowl River, and Big Bertha, the super tug, headed back to Mobile.

On its return from Bayou La Batre, the ferry brought a Sheriff's Department vehicle with a bullhorn on the roof. Four deputies accompanied the car. Coordinating with Randy Manning, they set out immediately urging people on the beaches to prepare for evacuation.

At one that afternoon, a few strands of wispy gray clouds dotted the sky. At two p.m. a light shower fell sporadically, the sound of it whispering through trees and brushing softly the roof of Manning's Garage. Here were the far-flung castoffs of the storm, driven by the earth's rotation, meandering hundreds of miles from the eye of Constance. Yet, Al knew the gentle rain would trigger a plunging barometer.

He stepped out of the garage into the drizzle and for a while watched Randy just across the road tying boats securely. Earlier in the day, Al had helped Lou nail plywood to the windows of the Pelican Pub, and before that Randy and he had done the same at the garage office. He and Doyle had long since sealed up his own house. Yet, Al had no faith in such precautions. He believed in fate. And when it came to nature, nothing so embodied fate as the weather.

————

All across the island, people tuned their radios and t.v.s to news and weather stations. At the

137

shore, few seemed concerned. Teenagers rushed into the growing waves with abandon.

"They say it's coming into Alabama," one told her friend.

"Great!" he answered. "I always wanted to be in a hurricane."

"No chance," another interjected. "They're gonna make you get off the island. They just said it on the radio. Mandatory ejaculation. "

"Evacuation, idiot."

Shortly after 2 p.m. the announcement came:

"Constance has turned to the northeast. She now appears headed toward Mobile, with a possible landfall between Biloxi, Mississippi, and Pensacola, Florida. That entire area is now under a hurricane *warning*. I repeat, this is not a watch but a formal *hurricane warning* from the National Weather Service. Constance, with winds gusting as high as one hundred twenty miles an hour, is traveling at fourteen miles per hour and is predicted to make landfall sometime Friday morning between Biloxi and Pensacola.

"This is a hurricane *warning*. All those living in low-lying or coastal areas, or along a river for at least seventy miles inland, are emphatically urged to evacuate. The governor of Alabama has issued an order to evacuate all coastal areas of that state. This is a *mandatory evacuation order for Alabamians*. The governors of Mississippi and Florida are expected to do the same at any moment."

An hour later, bumper-to-bumper traffic clogged Bienville Boulevard from Billy Goat Hole to a mile west of LeMoyne. Ferries had cut the round trip to Bayou La Batre to an hour and fifteen minutes, but the barge took two and a half hours. More than a thousand people in cars and on foot had been shuttled to the mainland on the ferry and barge. Several hundred others had fled in private boats. Three service boats from the oil rigs, which had long since been evacuated, stood by in the event they were needed, along with a Coast Guard cutter.

At Zechariah Ledbettter's store, the crush of customers was suffocating. Bread and milk had sold out days earlier, after the bridge collapsed. Now panicked shoppers rapidly cleared the shelves of soft drinks, batteries, lanterns, candles, matches, fuel, canned foods, ice. A minor scuffle broke out between two women over a can of tomato soup.

Back along Bienville Boulevard, Randy's volunteers had set up roadblocks in the west-bound lanes, heading away from the loading area. "We gotta keep them open for emergency traffic," Randy had ordered. Now he drove along the empty lanes with Al at his side counting the number of cars backed up in traffic across the grassy median in the east-bound lanes.

"One hundred sixty-seven," Al exclaimed. "No, Sixty-eight, sixty-nine—there's headlights still coming far as I can see, Randy."

"We'll never get them off the island in time—the sea'll be kicking up soon."

A sudden wind gust caught him by surprise, and pushed the truck onto the grassy shoulder. As quickly as the wind rose, it abated, and the rain fell quietly.

"It's a mathematical impossibility," Randy continued. "Time to refuel. Loading and unloading. Look, see if you can get some of them to leave their cars on the shoulder. Have them walk over here to the west-bound lane. We'll get a bus, shuttle them up to the Hole. There's plenty of boats there to take them to the mainland."

"You got it, boss," Al said. He pulled the yellow raincoat tight against his throat, tugged the rubber hat down over his ears, and opened the door.

Randy dropped the truck into low gear and headed back to the garage. For several minutes, he had been thinking about the garage, its cinder block walls the only refuge for perhaps hundreds of people. A single thought obsessed him. He would build a barrier wall, not to hold back a rising surge, but to prevent obstacles—even boats—from being hurled into the building.

Back in the yard, he phoned Lou Parrish at the Pelican Pub.

"You doing anything, Lou?"

"Sitting here in the dark waiting, praying it goes somewhere else. What else *can* I do?" Randy heard the despair in his voice.

"I need your help. There's a bus behind the Little Red Schoolhouse. There'll be people waiting in the median on Bienville east. I want you to pick them up and take them to Billy Goat Hole. You can use the west-bound lane. It's closed to traffic. Lou?"

"Yeah, I can do that. Nothing else to accomplish here. I'll be right over."

After Lou picked up the bus keys, Randy jogged out to the front-end loader. He tried to start it, but the battery was dead. He had another charging in the garage, and twenty minutes after his first attempt, Randy heard the rusty old machine groan, sputter, and come to life.

Cookie'll never believe this, he thought, as he dropped the bucket under a rusted old car engine. Just junk—wanted me to get rid of it, sell it for scrap. Well, maybe next week.

He drove the loader to the shoulder of the road, about twenty feet from the office door, and laid the bucket over. The motor tumbled out. Spinning the wheel, stomping the clutch, and throwing the gearshift into reverse, he raced back to the yard. An old bathtub, another engine, an empty one-hundred-gallon fuel tank, the body of a car burned in a fire. Some lifted, some nudged, all fell into place in a semi-circle guarding the Sound-facing side of the garage.

A refrigerator and a washing machine joined the barricade. He'd planned to use the compressor for something or other, and the motor in the washing machine for parts.

No man could live long enough to make use of all this junk, he thought. The absurdity of it made him smile. He licked at the raindrops around his lips, rubbed his hand across his forehead to remove a tuft of soggy hair from his eyes. Yes, he'd get rid of it all next week, clear it out of his life, make things simple again. He and Cookie would leave the island.

"Yahoo!" he exclaimed, and found himself laughing into a gusty wind.

━━━━━

"Damn it, Ruth, we warned everybody we could. Now you gotta get to the mainland!" Don shouted. He was standing in the living room of Ruth's condominium staring out at the wind-driven rain. He felt the building shiver.

"I've been taking care of myself for a hell of a long time. I don't need a daddy now."

He walked across the floor to her. She was frying some eggs in a pan. He put his hands on her shoulders. "Hon," he said, "you've never been in a hurricane, have you? When that thing hits, this whole condo could end up a pile of junk. One decent wave would take it out."

141

She spun around, her eyes reflecting the fury she felt. "You know what this is, don't you?" she demanded. "This is my husband's doing, this Constance shit. I don't know how, but he's behind it!"

Don pulled her to him. At first she resisted, then relaxed in his arms. "Let me take you to the ferry," he said softly.

"No, honey," Ruth answered, her voice gentle. "I'm not getting pushed around, not even by a hurricane."

Don sighed. He released her, and walked back to the window. "Sometimes you're really a pain in the neck, you know that, Ruth?"

"So I've been told."

"Well, I can see there's no reasoning with you. So let me put it this way. You're going with me to the garage. We're packing up some food, whatever else we need, and you're going with me. If I have to, I'll hog-tie you, gag you, and throw you over my shoulder. But I hope you'll just get in the car with me."

"That's what I been saying! I'm staying with you. I don't care where the hell it is. Here, the garage, the car, the beach—you name it."

———

Betsy Smith had awakened that morning to the evacuation order blaring from a car moving slowly along Bienville Boulevard. Her first thought was to leave the island immediately. She awakened Bill with a steaming cup of coffee and the words, "We should go, honey. Now. On the first ferry. I'm worried."

"Oh, Betsy," Bill groaned. He sat up and took the coffee from her, sipping it slowly. "Look out the window. The sun's out. Not even any waves to speak

142

of. The kids came to have fun. Let them play a while. There's plenty of time."

"Bill, the radio and television are talking about nothing but this storm. I don't want us anywhere around here if it comes our way."

"It's not gonna come our way. And so what if it does? We get to the ferry and in twenty minutes we're on the mainland."

Later that morning, she walked across the sand and climbed the steps to Abby's huge beach-side deck with its brass rails and planters filled with Spanish Bayonets. aloe vera and crepe myrtle. Wrought iron furniture rested on glazed mauve Italian tiles, the chairs cushioned with plush olive green pads. Here, on any given night, while the sun set below the horizon in a sky ablaze with color, Abby would throw her wild parties.

Betsy tried the handle of the double French door. As usual, it was unlocked. Still, she didn't step in but called from the deck, "Abby, are you decent?"

Only once had she walked in unannounced to discover Abby and two men, stark naked right there on the floor of the great room doing things she and Bill had never even imagined. She'd felt the flush of embarrassment from her face to her toes and spun back to the door with a wave of feigned nonchalance, calling over her shoulder, "Call me when you're... Well, whatever."

"It's okay, the coast is clear," Abby announced. As Betsy stepped into the great room, she added, "Except for those naked guys on your left."

Betsy turned with a start, but the room was empty. "Shame on you, Abby," she said, smiling. Abby sat at the kitchen counter in panties sipping coffee. Betsy took a cup and saucer from a cabinet and poured herself a cup. She pulled out a stool and sat next to Abby.

"So, how do rednecks have safe sex in Alabama?" Abby asked.

Betsy grimaced. "Is this going to be another one of your obscene jokes?"

"They spray paint the flanks of all the sheep that kick."

Betsy laughed and shook her head. "What am I going to do with you?" she asked.

"Love me. Just love me," Abby said, kissing Betsy's forehead. "Widow Jones hires a gay guy to help on the farm." Betsy groaned. "After a month, he asks the widow if he can have Saturday night off to go to town. She says it's okay, but he's got to be home by nine. Ten-thirty, he finally sneaks up the stairs to his room. Widow Jones suddenly bursts in on him and finds him jerking—masturbating.

"'How wasteful!' she yells. 'Come here, take off my shoes.'" He obeys. 'Take off my dress.' He does. 'Take off my slip...and stockings...and my garter belt.' He does everything she says without a word.

"'Now take off my bra,' she snaps, 'And don't you ever borrow my clothes again!'"

Betsy laughed heartily. "Oh, that's just awful!" she declared.

Abby laughed, too. "You know," she said. "Beneath that prudish exterior, there's a good-hearted, fun-loving human being."

"I *am* a fun-loving person. Who was it pushed you into the mud when you were showing off your fancy new dress? There you sat sputtering—I thought that was hysterical."

"But you didn't think it was funny when I smashed that rotten tomato into your head for pay-back."

"Well, with hindsight, I think that was pretty funny, too." She reached for Abby's hand.

"We were a real team," Abby said.

"We still are, and always will be. And I want that to be a long time, which is why I'm here. I want you to come back to Mobile with us today."

Abby pulled her hand away and moved to the window overlooking the Gulf. "I'm not leaving," she said softly.

"Oh, Abby. For heaven's sake, why not?"

"Number one, I'm as safe right here as I would be in Mobile. This house was *designed* to withstand a hurricane. God knows what would happen to that dump Kendell Hall if a hurricane hit it. It could collapse on top of me."

"That dump, as you call it, has survived probably a dozen hurricanes since it was built. It's a fort."

"Number two: Most of the time I'm bored to death with life—"

"You? Abby Marwick, partying every night in the week practically, having non-stop sex orgies, traveling wherever she wants, whenever she wants, buying—"

"Don't you understand?" Abby shouted. "None of it means anything. I'm not like you. I don't have kids and a husband—well, forget the husband."

"Sometimes I'd like to."

"You have something to hold your life together, some purpose or whatever you call it. No, I'm staying here. I'm going to see what a hurricane is all about. In fact, you know what I'm going to do? I'm going to have a hurricane party!"

Betsy crossed the room to where Abby stood half nude at the window. She put her arms around her friend. "Abby Marwick, if anything were ever to happen to you..." She threw her head back and stared at the ceiling, her mouth open. "I just don't know how I could face that. I just don't know."

———

At noon, Betsy pleaded with Bill to pack, pointing to the eerie-looking yellow sky. He laughed.

"That's the sun behind some clouds, that's all," he said. "Look, we'll start the barbecue, cook up some hotdogs and hamburgers. After that there's plenty of time."

"Bill—"

"Look, I paid for a *month*, not four *days*!" he shouted. "If we have to leave, we have to leave, but not till we have a little more fun. Is that clear?" He riveted her with an angry glare.

Betsy grew silent.

At two that afternoon, the kids persuaded Bill to build them a sand castle. By four they had the car packed and ready to go. It had already begun raining, and when they reached LeMoyne Avenue and Bienville Boulevard, they confronted a line of traffic.

"Oh, Lord," Betsy whispered.

"No problem," Bill assured her. "Probably an accident. Things'll get moving in a minute."

Al knocked on the driver's side window, the rain running down his face.

"No chance getting on the ferry today," he said. "Not if you want to take your car. We can run you down to Billy Goat Hole. Plenty of boats there. Just pull off on the shoulder and—"

"Leave my car here?" Bill exclaimed. "Not on your life. Who's to look out for it? Vandals,

146

thieves, they'd have a field day with it. Nothing doing. Where I go this car goes."

"Well," Al said, "it's about where it's going for the next couple of days, if you ask me."

"Is there a shelter?" Betsy asked, leaning across her husband.

"Yes, ma'am. Head north up that there street four blocks, till you get to the gas station. Hang a left, and you'll see a big cinder block building, Manning's Garage. That's it there. Plenty of room to park your car," Al added, scowling.

———

Wind gusts along the island's Gulf shore assaulted Doyle Donahue in sudden, fitful bursts. He had climbed the dune to sense the sea's mood. Although he lacked Al's instinct, he had spent his adult life on the water, and understood it.

From where he stood, the surf blurred with the darkness and rain. He trudged down the dune and toward the angry sea until he could see to the west the lights of the Isle Dauphine Restaurant. There, the water level had risen several feet above the high tide line. Four-foot waves spilled over the asphalt parking lot.

He climbed back over the dune, bounded down to the road, and hurried north toward Bienville Boulevard. He paused for a moment at Al's cottage before moving on.

He'd go to Randy's garage. It would be risky. Somebody had said a sheriff's deputy was watching the *Barbara*. He would have to chance arrest, and, after all, he deserved it. But he'd lived through a miracle. His life had been spared for a reason. That's what Al had said. Maybe this was it. Maybe he could help. Randy would find something for him to do.

The streets of the old village had turned to slippery brown mud. The houses were shadows, their windows boarded, with only a single speck of light peeking through a crack here and there. His own house, when he passed it, seemed vulnerable by comparison. The windows would be blown out, the furniture floating in four feet of muddy water come Saturday. He didn't care. Saturday would be another lifetime. By then, or Sunday, he'd probably be in jail, maybe even dead. Whoever wants the house can have it, he thought.

He approached the intersection at DeSoto cautiously, certain a sheriff's deputy would be stationed at the tug. Seeing no one, he hurried to the vessel. Someone, probably Randy had tied it securely, cross ties reaching from the bow and stern on both the port and starboard sides.

He studied the vessel. It showed no signs of damage. Even now, it seemed to him the most beautiful vessel in the world.

"You work seven days a week. I never see you," his wife had said. He told her it was the price they had to pay. He'd sacrificed everything.

He'd sacrificed too much. Not for a second did he think she'd actually leave, and when she did the boat seemed so unimportant. Now, gazing through the darkness at the glistening rain-slicked hull, realizing he would never pilot *Barbara* again, he felt the physical ache of great sorrow.

He turned and, leaning into the wind, struggled to the garage.

"Where the hell have you been?" Randy exclaimed. Don, Ruth, Lou, and several others shouted his name and rushed to greet him.

"Heard all kinds of stuff about you," said Don. "One says you drowned, another you hanged yourself. A guy from New Orleans said the Mafia blew your brains out for smuggling drugs. Knowing you, I believed every one of them!" The crowd laughed.

"Where you been?" Randy asked again.

"Can't tell you that. Might get somebody in trouble."

"Good enough," Ruth said. "The real question is, have you been eating right?" Doyle shrugged.

"Well, you come on in here and I'll feed you good!" Ruth said. She grabbed his arm and led him to the area she had arranged as a makeshift kitchen.

Randy sat down across from Doyle. "It could get pretty bad," he said.

"I figured. That's what Al said. It's spooky the way he can tell about such things. Where is he, anyway?"

Randy turned his eyes from Doyle's. He shook his head. "He was out on Bienville toward Billy Goat Hole. Last I heard from him, the ferry was gone and not coming back, and he was trying to get traffic turned around, directing them back here. He was calling in here non-stop for a while, said there was an accident and water rising. I can't get him to answer the CB for love or money now. I hope he gets out of there before it's too late."

Doyle chomped half a hotdog and roll in a single bite. "You don't have to worry about Al," he said. "I seen him get hit with an eight-foot-high wave, thrown clear up on the highway, stand up and walk away. And the guy never learned to swim! Of course, he wasn't a cripple then. Had two good arms.

Come to think of it, he was twenty years younger, too."

"Feel like getting some fresh air?" Randy asked Doyle.

"Yeah, whatever you need."

"Get on over to Zach's store for storm lanterns and flashlights. And batteries and oil. We'll need twenty or thirty lanterns. Take money from the desk. Old Ledbetter won't sell a toothpick on credit unless you're a native."

He turned to Don. "How's it coming?"

Don studied Randy's face. "Damned if you're not having a blast with all this," he said. "Look at him, Ruth. Look at his eyes." He burst out singing, "Irish eyes are *smiling*."

"Manning's not Irish," Ruth said.

———

Early that evening, the entire Gulf coast was abuzz with activity. Thousands of vehicles from the islands and low-lying areas brought northbound highway traffic to a crawl. On Highway 65 north out of Mobile, authorities used southbound lanes for northbound traffic

Supermarket shelves emptied quickly of critical supplies—bottled water, canned fruits and vegetables, lamp oil, milk, bread. Procrastinators raced to lumberyards for plywood and to hardware stores for nails, flashlights, batteries, oil lamps. As supplies dwindled, prices increased dramatically.

On Dauphin Island, Zach Ledbetter began doubling prices of every item he sold.

Some people panicked. Others, like Betsy, chose to face the coming hours with resigned serenity, hoping her faith would hold out when she really needed it.

Still others anticipated the storm with eagerness and exhilaration. Among them were Randy Manning and Abby Marwick.

CHAPTER XV

It was 7 p.m. One hundred fifteen miles southwest of Dauphin Island, the Gulf, from its surface to a height of twelve miles, was still and silent in the eye of Constance. With a diameter of twenty miles, it formed an almost perfect circle of rippling water and cloudless sky.

But in the wall of that eye, shards of rain slashed at one hundred thirty miles an hour in ceaseless fury. For one hundred miles in every direction, gale force winds drove scud over the sea. Rain and wind gusts reached as far west as Galveston and east to Panama City. By 10 p.m., New Orleans, west of the storm and spared the severest winds, cringed under torrential rains driven from the northeast in the storm's cyclonic counter-clockwise circulation.

———

Ferryboat Captain John Randall made the announcement at seven-fifteen p.m. One of the mates pulled a chain across the loading area and fastened it in place, and Randall shouted into the megaphone, "This is it. Our last trip. Too much surge, and the wind's getting nasty. We'll ride it out in Fowl River." The barge and other ferry had already holed up at Bayou La Batre.

"You can't do that!" someone yelled.

"You're leaving us here to die!"

Chased by a chorus of shouts, the captain disappeared into the pilothouse. The mates cast off the lines and the engines roared. Someone threw a rock at the ferry. It bounced off the steel hull like a rubber ball. The ship eased into the channel, the wake rippling in the darkness, four-foot waves slapping at its sides.

By then, the entire press corps of hundreds had abandoned the island. Like a swarm of bees, the helicopters had lifted into the air, hovered, and flown off to the mainland. Those who had arrived in boats scurried back to safety by the same means, the stragglers pounding through unsettlingly high waves and strong winds. With the last journalist gone, Al thought he felt the island shudder and settle.

Lou Parrish had driven the old school bus along the two-mile stretch from LeMoyne and Bienville to Billy Goat Hole and back six times. He'd carried perhaps two hundred fifty people to the ferry docks and escape, and now he would pick up those huddled in the median and transport them to the garage. He drove slowly, peering through the rain-drenched windshield.

Farther ahead, Al moved from car to car. "Ferry's not coming back," he yelled at each window. "No other boats, either. They're all headed for shelter. Might as well turn around, just go on over to Manning's Garage. They'll show you where up at the intersection."

Using his flashlight as a pointer, and waving with his hook, he directed the traffic across the median into the westbound lanes.

Farther to the west, other drivers saw the headlights moving toward them from the Hole. Some had been waiting in line for hours, and now, realizing the futility of delaying any longer, they maneuvered out of the traffic and into the median strip.

At most points, the grass divider was level with the road surface, but at one stretch between LeMoyne and Hernando the grass dipped gradually before rising again. Here, several cars bogged down, slithering sideways before gaining sufficient traction to sprint up onto the asphalt.

Near the western end of the line of traffic, Jessica and Norman sat in the gray Thunderbird, the engine off and the windshield opaque with the condensed moisture of their breath. Periodically, Norman wiped it clean with his handkerchief and turned on the windshield wiper. He felt the car shudder in a particularly violent wind gust. Rain pelted the passenger window where Jessica sat, separated from the Gulf by a few hundred yards of loblolly pines. A dead branch from one of them screeched across the Thunderbird's hood like a javelin.

"Damn," said Norman.

Jessica smiled. She reached around his neck, gripped his shoulder muscles and massaged them.

"You're tense," she said.

"It's my own fault. I was late getting to the motel. I couldn't think what to do to protect my boat. I loosened the lines so it could float higher on the waves.

Through the moisture on the windshield, Norman saw the glare of oncoming headlights. He wiped the windshield clear. "Oh, that's great," he said with a sigh. "You see that? The ferry's gone for the duration."

Jessica looked at him somberly. "What does *that* mean?" she asked.

Norman heard the first rumble of thunder in the distance. "Water's probably getting too rough. Those cars are headed to Randy's garage, I guess. Not to their houses, I hope—not if they're west of here. We might as well head to the garage."

Norman eased the Thunderbird down the gentle slope of the median and through the mud. The oncoming traffic was a considerable distance away, so he pressed the accelerator and moved smoothly toward the asphalt.

At the same moment, the car behind him spun into the mud to his left, fishtailed, its rear right fender ramming the rear left of the Thunderbird. Overcompensating, the driver spun the wheel to the right, plunging into the front of Norman's car.

Brakes squealed. The lead car in oncoming traffic skidded sideways and collided with the passenger side of the Thunderbird.

The car behind it spun off onto the shoulder and hit a tree. While Norman and Jessica watched and listened in astonishment, the tearing metal and breaking glass continued like a roll of thunder into the distance.

Norman threw up his hands, dropped them to his side. He shook his head. Turning to Jessica, he started to speak, then closed his mouth and stared out through the windshield. Jessica rested her hand on his.

When he turned to her, she smiled. Her smile broadened. She laughed, continued laughing until tears dampened her face. Norman began laughing, too.

"Would you please tell me what's so funny?" he asked.

"You!" she gasped. "If you...have a guardian angel... he...ought to be...shot!"

"After every feather is slowly and painfully plucked from his wings!"

The scene on DeSoto in front of Manning's Garage seemed to Lou Parrish, who sat behind the wheel of the school bus, hopelessly chaotic. Traffic had come to a standstill. People swarmed along the road from the east and west, lines of them snaking around stalled cars, some carrying umbrellas blown inside out, others with rain slickers tightened under their chins, a few bare-chested adolescents mingled in the chaos. With every fresh gust, hats skipped through headlight beams and sailed northwestward into the sound. Through the windshield, Lou saw Randy Manning up ahead directing traffic. Drivers from both directions were trying to move through the narrow gate simultaneously, and Randy was attempting to stagger them.

One driver coming from the west attempted to pass the garage and go on to LeMoyne Avenue, but Randy's barricade of junk cluttered the eastbound shoulder. Lou's bus occupied the westbound lane. Car horns blared. Drivers wound down their windows and cursed each other.

Randy came running toward the bus. Lou cranked down the window. The rain drenched him almost instantly.

"Lou, can't you pull off onto the shoulder somehow? We gotta keep things moving."

"I'll see what I can do." He cranked up the window, dropped the bus into gear, and eased it forward. He stopped a few inches from the bumper of a white Plymouth Reliant.

Randy rapped on the driver's side window.

"What?" Bill Smith barked, refusing to roll down the window.

"You're going to have to pull up on the shoulder," Randy shouted. "We have to get the bus out of the lane, get traffic moving."

"I'm putting my car behind that fence over there where it's safe."

156

"You're not putting your car anywhere unless we move traffic. Please—pull off on the shoulder and ahead twenty feet or so."

"Please, Bill," Betsy Smith said to her husband.

"Tell the guy in front of me to do it." Bill Smith turned away, ignoring Randy.

"Listen, you son of a bitch," Randy exploded, pounding his fist on the car roof, "get this piece of shit off the road now, or that bus is gonna move it for you. Lou!"

"Children, cover your ears," Betsy Smith ordered.

Bill Smith pointed his finger at Randy and glowered, but turned the wheel and drove off the road.

Inside the garage, Don and Ruth sat behind a long table, their backs to the office door. To their right were the small kitchen and cot, and the toilet. Don had hung a tablecloth where a door should have been. He said, as he and Ruth watched the endless procession enter the cavernous building, "It's like a world-wide refugee operation." In fact there were Creole families, Cajuns, blacks, Hispanics, whites, children, teens, parents, grandparents. They were dressed in jeans, slacks, shorts, bathing suits, skirts. Rain-drenched faces reflected numb bewilderment.

Once in the building, the people spread out, meandering in every direction between rows of cots and mattresses, finding unoccupied areas, staking them with suitcases, wet clothing, shoes and socks. Many of those who had brought dry clothes stood in line at the toilet. Others lay sheets over the mattresses and crawled beneath them to change.

They spoke softly, and rarely to strangers. Their voices created a rhythmic hum, rising and falling like the waves of the Gulf. Among themselves they shared questions and expectations. After a while, growing more confident, they looked around and nodded to others whom they recognized.

"They look like zombies," Ruth told Don. "Let's get that coffee pot going."

Don went to the office and unpacked two large coffee makers, each with a twenty-cup capacity. He poured coffee into the sieves, filled the pots with water, and plugged them into separate outlets.

"Who needs so much coffee?" he'd asked Ruth when she told him to load the pots into the Cadillac.

"We had parties. The rug man would invite his whole family. And the family wasn't just relatives, if you know what I mean. I know how much coffee people drink."

———

When Lou Parrish stepped out of the bus into the downpour, he found himself surrounded by a throng of bare-chested young men and halter-topped women.

"It's wild, man!"

"Never been in a hurricane before!"

"Come on, Lou, open the cafe. Plenty of time before it hits."

"It's boarded up!" Lou yelled.

"Not the door, just the windows," a woman yelled.

"Come on, Lou—just for an hour."

"Then you'll get your butts over to the garage?"

"Yeah!"

"Sure!"

"All right." The crowd screamed its approval.

———

Betsy Smith, Bill, and the children sloshed around the traffic, through the gates, across the muddy, rain-swept yard and into the garage, blending into the anonymous crowd. Bill sought out the mattresses still available, testing several until he found one he felt was satisfactory.

"Here we go—this is our home for the night," he announced, tossing a suitcase onto the mattress.

He looked around him. "This place is a shambles," he said. "Look at them, still coming in. It's like a field hospital in a war zone. They should've planned better than this. We'll probably come down with dysentery, or the plague." He whispered to Betsy, "Whatever you do, don't let them find out about the food we got. There could be a riot. We could get killed."

Betsy stared at him dryly. "You worry about the food," she said. "I'm worried about Abby."

"That tramp?"

"That's not very Christian, Bill. Jesus forgave the prostitute and condemned those who were self-satisfied religionists."

"Where'd you get such a notion?"

"From a radical book, the Bible, Matthew, chapter seven, verses twenty-one through twenty-three. Right now, I'd say you have a pretty good chance of going to hell before morning if these walls don't protect us. You just watch the children—who would be safe asleep in their beds back in Mobile right now if you had listened to me."

She spoke softly, but Bill saw the anger in her eyes and said nothing. He watched her weave her way through the crowd.

"Daddy found the best mattress of all, didn't he?" he asked the children.

Maybe she changed her mind, Betsy thought. She searched hundreds of faces several times as she pressed through the crowd. Finally she approached Don and Ruth. "Have you seen Abby Marwick?" she asked. They hadn't. In the office, Doyle suggested maybe Randy, still directing traffic, might help. She refastened her raincoat, pulling the collar up around her neck, and stepped through the outer office door into a now steadily blowing wind.

A tall man in a yellow slicker, the one who'd told Bill to move the car, was shouting and waving a flashlight.

"Are you Randy?" she yelled. He nodded. "I'm looking for Abby Marwick."

"Said she was having a hurricane party at her place. Even she can't be that nuts. Check the pub." He shook his head and turned back to the traffic.

Even from where she stood in the street, Betsy could feel the thump of base notes from the speakers. She pressed her lips together firmly and ran toward the steps to the second floor of what she'd heard was Dauphin Island's premier den of iniquity.

Still, she wasn't prepared for the crowd of voluptuous, nearly naked people who confronted her. Several women wore halters overflowing with breasts. The men were bare chested and barefoot, wearing only crotch-hugging shorts. With mouth wide, she watched them gyrate to the pulse of the speakers.

160

She lifted her gaze from their bodies to their faces, and even walked among them. The heat they radiated made her light-headed. Finally, she saw Lou Parrish.

"Sir," she said, trying to avoid his stunning blue eyes, "have you seen Abby Marwick this evening?"

"No, ma'am," Lou answered. "She called here a few times, though. Invited some of the guys over to her place."

"Oh, no!"

"Don't worry, they're not going. They're not the swiftest crowd we ever had, but they're not *that* stupid."

"I'm worried about *Abby*!" Betsy turned and started to the door.

"No need, ma'am," Lou called after her. "That place of hers is *guaranteed* to withstand one-hundred-fifty-mile-an-hour winds."

Pride goeth before destruction, Betsy thought. She raced down the stairs from the Pelican Pub and jogged past the yellow school bus to the Plymouth Reliant. The engine started immediately. She pulled out into DeSoto, driving west, then south to Bienville, and west again through darkness and slashing rain. To her left, much closer than she recalled, she heard the roaring waves of the Gulf.

Since childhood, Betsy had been the mature, responsible one, always looking out for her friend. And she was determined to do it again now, come heck or high water. There was still time.

———

Forty minutes later, Randy stood in DeSoto waving the battery-operated flashlight as it cycled between red and white flashes. Cars now approached only sporadically.

"Pull in as tight as you can," he told each driver. "We'll worry about getting out when the time comes."

Occasionally, stragglers still stumbled along the road toward the garage. Fathers and mothers carried their children. An elderly couple supported each other. A group of college students headed first for the Pelican Pub. Then, finding that Lou was closing up, crossed the street.

"What's the deal?" a muscular young man yelled to Randy.

"Stick around, you'll find out."

"Hell, we got a party to go to!" another responded. "Abby Marwick's throwing a Hurricane Blast."

Randy shook his head. "The west end's probably under water by now," he said. "You'll stall out and drown."

"I'm not going," one of the girls said.

"Me neither."

"So what're we supposed to do?" the muscular boy asked, throwing wide his arms.

"You can try surviving," Randy said sarcastically. "Why don't you go inside and get bored?"

"Makes sense to me."

In the garage, groups formed around several portable TV's. The same report from the National Oceanic and Atmospheric Administration meteorologist was being broadcast simultaneously on all local stations:

"Hurricane Constance is now at 28° north latitude, 89° west longitude, and is moving north-northeast directly toward Mobile, Alabama, at

35 miles an hour. Constance remains a category three hurricane, with sustained winds at 125 miles an hour, and gusts reaching to 160.

"Low-lying waterfront communities all along the coast have been evacuated by order of the governors of Louisiana, Mississippi, Alabama, and Florida. But the nation's attention has been focused during the last 24 hours on Dauphin Island, a quiet vacation community where, on Monday of this week, a runaway coal barge destroyed the only bridge to the mainland. As a result, emergency evacuation efforts have been underway for two days, using ferries, barges, and vessels supplied by oil companies, the Coast Guard and hundreds of private volunteer boat owners.

"All rescue efforts were discontinued early this evening, however, because of strong winds and rough seas preceding Hurricane Constance. Authorities on the island have reported by VHF that, through random searches of properties and head counts, an estimated 500 people are still stranded on the island, some remaining in their homes, hundreds huddled in a cinder block garage, and, tragically, an unknown number apparently stranded in their cars. Wind speed will continue to increase throughout the night on the little barrier island, with a storm surge expected to reach 15 to 20 feet, leaving much of the island under water. The hurricane's eye is expected to make landfall late tomorrow morning. Stay tuned for continual updates."

The children, in a festive mood, chased each other between rows of mattresses, squealing and shouting until their parents hushed them. Even the adults, more relieved in the convivial atmosphere, now chattered with holiday-like enthusiasm.

"They say it already sank a cruise ship out in the Caribbean," someone said over the rain drumming on the metal roof.

"Who's 'they?'"

"Barbara Anne."

"Barbara Anne hasn't a lick of sense."

"We couldn't have waited another minute— the water was coming up the steps. Lucky we're just renting for the week. We packed everything in the car."

"Well, our house was built solid. I saw to it. It's survived three hurricanes so far. I guess one more won't make much difference."

"If I had my choice, I'd be anywhere but here right now. But I don't. So I'm not."

"I've never done a hurricane before. If you ask me it's an adventure, something to write about at school this fall."

"If you live."

Just then, a large hunk of debris, hurled by the wind, slammed into the roof. Children screamed.

"All right, all right," Ruth bellowed from behind the table at the front of the garage, "we'll have none of that nonsense." She stood and walked to the queen-sized mattress she and Don had brought from the condo and placed beside the table. "Now, come up here, boys and girls," she shouted. "Take your shoes and socks off. Sit on this nice big bed, and I'll tell you a story."

As the children came forward, Don gave Ruth a puzzled look.

"I was a school teacher a hundred years ago when I was young," Ruth explained.

Giggling, jostling, the children gathered on the mattress, the older ones in back, the younger ones forward. Ruth pulled up a chair and sat facing them.

"This is a story about a hurricane," she said with mystery in her voice. "One just like Constance, who's going to visit us tonight. And it's a *scary* story, but this is what you must remember—it will have a happy ending."

Across the room, one woman said to another, "We live just a few houses away, and I haven't seen you in *ages*!"

"Isn't it the truth—it takes a funeral or natural disaster to bring people together."

At that moment, the power failed. The cavernous room plunged into darkness. A child cried, "Momma!"

"No, now—don't be afraid," exclaimed Ruth. "This is part of our *story*!" She whispered to Don, "Get some lanterns lit."

She turned back to the children, pointing a flashlight at her face. "All the people had gathered in Randy's garage, where they knew they would be safe. And there was a very brilliant man among them, Don Long, who—" The crowd laughed.

"As I was saying, a *very* smart man who had planned ahead for just such an occurrence. Low and behold, he remembered to carry an oil lamp, and, by bringing forth a cigarette lighter, he ignited the wick and lit up the entire room."

She paused, waiting. After several seconds, she began again. "He brought forth a magic cigarette lighter. I say, a *magic lighter*!" Again the crowd laughed. Suddenly, the lamp glowed and spread its weak light throughout the building. Everyone, including the youngsters, applauded.

Outside, the street was finally empty except for a few people on foot. Suddenly, as Randy guided the stragglers toward the building, the island was enveloped in darkness—floods on the Pelican Pub, streetlights, house lights in the nearby old village, garage office lights—all failed.

Randy headed to the cinder block shed behind the garage where the generator had been installed. Wiping the rain from his eyes, he began jogging, tripped, sprawled in mud. He reached the shed and forced open the door open against the wind. In moments the generator kicked in. He saw the glow of light through the cracks and holes in the sheet metal siding, and heard cheers.

Running back to the street, he picked up a small group of stragglers from the Pelican Pub and led them back to the office.

"What a sight!" Don exclaimed. Water poured from Randy's slicker, his nose and chin, washing away the mud he'd fallen into. As he took off the gear, Bill Smith rushed in from outside, as drenched as Randy, his face reflecting despair.

"I'm worried sick about my wife," he blurted. "The car's gone!"

Randy recognized him, considered telling him to go to hell, but asked, "Where would she go?"

"I think she went back for our neighbor, Abby Marwick. You know her? That Marwick woman's nothing... If anything happens to Betsy..." He brushed his hand across his face and turned away. "Why would Betsy do such a thing for a woman like that, anyway?" he sobbed. "She's out there." He turned back to Randy, his eyes pleading. "I gotta get her. That woman, Ruth somebody, promised to watch my kids. Please, can you help?"

Randy stared at the other man pensively. Finally, he asked, "You think she's at Abby's?"

"I hope to God she made it, not that she's stuck someplace."

"Okay, come on." Randy put his yellow raincoat back on, snapped the strap holding his hat in place, and the two lunged into the storm.

———

Half a block from Doyle's house in the old village, Randy stopped the truck. Although the headlights pierced the downpour for little more than ten feet, he and Bill Smith saw the lane was flooded. The first floors of the houses were already half filled with rising water.

"It's downhill from here, Bill," Randy said. "Another three inches and the truck's dead in the water." Bill Smith said nothing. He sat shaking his head.

They had already tried to reach Bienville Boulevard along LeMoyne, but the rush of water had made it impossible. The lane through the old village was the only alternative, and now that, too, had proved futile. Randy turned the truck around and headed back to the garage.

"What am I going to do?" Bill pleaded.

"Why didn't you leave this afternoon like you were told?" Randy said coldly.

"I…I…Oh, God!" Bill threw up his hands and wept.

FRIDAY

CHAPTER XVI

At one a.m. Abby Marwick stood in a white frilly bra and panties in the center of her great room facing the patio doors and deck. She could see nothing but rain driving angrily against the glass. When the gusts faltered for a second, she realized the forty yards of sparkling white sand had become seething waves rumbling toward the steps of her deck.

She went to the wall and turned the dimmer switch until the overhead lights blazed, and pressed some buttons on a console. Loud music blasted from speakers throughout the house. She stumbled to the wet bar and poured another glass of Absolut over ice.

Lowering herself unsteadily into the chair next to the phone, she dialed the Pelican Pub. After eight rings, she hung up.

"Where the hell are they?" she screamed. "I'm having a goddamn party and nobody's here." She stood and walked in a wobbly circle around the room, then sat at the phone again. After two rings, Lou Parrish answered.

"Manning's," he said.

"Lou, baby, this is Abby. Where *is* everybody. I'm havin' a pardy, but nobody's here. 'Cept me, 'course. How else could I be talkin' to ya?" she laughed sloppily.

"Everybody's here in the garage," Lou told her. "There's no way anyone could get out there even if they wanted to, and they don't. The whole island's under water, just about. I hope you'll be all right."

"Don't you go worryin' none about me, Louie, baby," she said and slammed the phone down. "Abby can take care of herself just fine," she told the room, and gulped her drink.

A loud pounding on the door facing the boulevard aroused her. She shut off the music.

"Ha!" she exclaimed. "We're havin' a pardy after all." She stumbled along the wide corridor into the library and threw open the rear door.

Betsy Smith, her hair matted across her face, clutching her shoes, stumbled inside. Abby slammed the door shut.

"What the hell're *you* doin' here?" Abby demanded in amazement. "Where're your kids?"

"They're all right. They're with Bill at the garage. I came to get you, Abby."

"You came—you outta your mind? For me? Why?"

"Abby Marwick, you're a fool, but not a damned fool—not yet, anyway. I'm...I'm not going to let you slip away from me like this."

Abby gasped. Shaking her head, she turned and stumbled back through the corridor to the great room, Betsy following. "No," Abby said, slumping into the sofa, "don't talk like that. You mustn't care!" She began sobbing. "Everybody I cared about..."

A moment later, she wiped her face dry with both hands. "You're a good kid, Betsy, but what you gotta unnerstand is, this place'll survive hunnred-an'-fifty-mile-an-hour winds. Never been a wave could knock it down. Tha's *guaranteed* by the archi...archi...architect."

"I'm sick of hearing guaranteed, guaranteed. What about the glass?"

"Steel roll-down shutters for every winnow in the house, north, south, east, west, south. Strong's an iron wall. I'm tellin' ya this place is impregna...na...ble."

At that moment, all over the island, darkness descended.

In Abby's home, emergency battery-powered lamps produced eerie pools of light in every room and on the deck facing the Gulf. The two women listened in silence to the howling wind and crashing waves.

"Oh, tha's great," Abby said. "Tha's just wonnerful."

"What?"

"The electricity's out—can't you see? The shutters— they're all electric!"

"Don't you have a generator?"

"A generator, yes. Gasoline, no! I forgot. I forgot!"

"Well, we'll just crank them manually." Betsy started toward the patio door.

First they heard the thumping on the deck. Then, bursting from the darkness, a metal chair tumbled across the planks, rose up, and crashed through the patio door. Glass flew everywhere. The chair sailed across the room, smashed into the wet bar and fell beside the women. Shards of glass lay all around them.

"This is crazy," Abby said. "Okay, les get outta here." She headed for the library and front door.

"Abby, that's not possible."

"Wha' da ya mean?"

"The water's so deep on the road my car flooded out. I waded and swam the last hundred yards. We're here for the ride. I think we should pray."

"Pray?" Abby scoffed. She erupted in mocking laughter. "I haven' prayed in years. I used ta pray. What good 'id do? They still get sick, die. I don' even believe there's a God, and if there is, He—maybe it's a She—She don't care one teensy weensy bit about Abby Marwick. She don't listen ta nobody's prayers. Maybe She's deaf. Maybe—"

An enormous crash burst from the back of the house, shaking the whole structure and throwing Abby to her knees next to Betsy at the sofa.

"I'm not gonna pray," she said emphatically, adding, "That don't mean you shouldn't."

———

In those early morning hours, battles were waged and lost all over the island. Jake Martin and his crew at Little Dauphin Bay Marina had been working since midday, stabilizing the boats in their slips with double bow and stern springs and lines, making sure fenders were in place, pulling boats in the most vulnerable slips out onto their trailers. Yet, the surge in some cases had already made a mockery of their efforts, ripping cleats loose, snapping lines, driving debris through hulls.

Earlier, back at the garage, a volunteer named Bubba Joe had replaced Lou Parrish at the steering wheel of the bus, sent out to pick up another load of stranded motorists along Bienville Boulevard east. He got as far as the boulevard when, even with his windshield wipers at high speed, the driving rain obscured his vision. In a panic, he jammed down the brake peddle. The bus slid off the road into a drainage ditch. The intersection was already beginning to flood when Bubba Joe climbed out the driver's side window and struggled back to the garage.

Norman held Jessica in his arms. He had pondered their circumstances for more than an hour, had considered trying to make it back to Randy's garage, but had decided against it because conditions were already too dangerous. Plodding blindly through flooded roads, they could easily step into a culvert and be swept into the Gulf. Besides, he thought, Randy wouldn't leave so many stranded on this particularly vulnerable stretch of road. Someone would come along to help if they'd remain patient.

"It's like the end of the world," Jessica said. "What an irony, to survive that bridge only to die in a hurricane the same week."

Norman caressed her hair. "You're not going to die," he said, "and neither am I." Yet, he knew it wasn't impossible. The road would certainly flood, filling the hollow where the Thunderbird rested. They might drown. A tree limb could crash through the windshield and kill them.

Gently, he took her face in his hands.

The door to Randy's garage flew open and he and Bill Smith, dripping wet, stumbled inside.

"Look, I know this island," Randy shouted. "If we'd 've tried driving through that cut, with the water moving that fast, we'd 've ended up in the Mississippi Sound and been no good to nobody 'cause we'd be dead."

"We can't just abandon her," Bill sobbed.

"Nobody's abandoning nobody," Randy said. "I'll come up with something."

By two that Friday morning, with Jessica and Norman sleeping in each other's arms in the Thunderbird, the water on Bienville Boulevard rose to seep under the car's doors. Through the barrage of wind and debris assailing the vehicle, both slept comfortably, but with the first screech of metal against the driver's side window, Jessica awakened.

"Norman, someone's out there!" she exclaimed.

"Where?"

She pointed to the driver's side window.

"Who is it?" Norman demanded.

"Me, Al," the voice roared over the wind. "You can't stay here. Another hour, these cars'll be flooded. It'll be too late! We gotta try getting to the shell mounds. Nothing higher on this island except that dune by Randy's place and the rise by the garage. I got a couple lines formed out here, maybe fifty of us. Come on out and grab somebody's hand so you don't get lost. Just brace yourself for the wind."

Norman took a flashlight from the glove compartment and stepped from the car into three feet of water. He clutched the door and leaned hard into the wind. Jessica slipped under the steering wheel.

"Watch it, water's deep," Norman yelled. Gingerly she thrust herself from the car, clinging to him. The wind whipped her long hair furiously.

With effort, Norman pushed the door to the Thunderbird closed, lit the flashlight, and led Jessica toward the line.

Al cupped his one hand around his mouth and yelled, "Hold onto each other—don't let go. Keep on the road. The shoulder drops away sharp in some places. Pass it along."

They heard Al shouting in the opposite direction. His voice seemed to drop like lead weights, but the message was repeated by others.

Finally, Al began moving through the water. Jessica held Norman's arm and an anonymous hand. Norman kept his flashlight trained on Al.

The line moved slowly, weaving around a vehicle, over debris. Peering ahead, Jessica saw, as through a frosted pane, the diffused glow of the flashlight Al had hung around his neck. It was moving north into the woods, parallel with LeMoyne.

"Next time let's do something less exotic," Jessica shouted.

"I don't believe in boring my dates," Norman answered.

From farther back in the line, they heard a woman's voice: "No, you can't cut across there, the water's too deep. Come back, Jerry!"

"Let him go. Here, grab my hand. Come on, quick!"

A man screamed, and a woman shrieked, "Jerry!"

"Come on, lady. He's on his own. Maybe he'll be all right." The wind overwhelmed the woman's sobs.

Norman squeezed Jessica's hand. She tightened her hold on him.

———

Silently Al spoke to the spirits. It was common knowledge that the shell mounds belonged to them. The dead were buried there, the ancient rulers. Before that, the mounds may have been the site of an open air temple where, in Mayan-like rituals, hearts were ripped from living flesh. Here, perhaps five thousand years ago, people worshipped in holy orgies, or prayed to thunder and lightning. Tonight his future and these people's would rest in the hands of the spirits and their sacred ground. Would they find this human presence sacrilege? He himself had always been too afraid to visit them.

Yet, he had no hope now but the mounds, for Al had survived three hurricanes, and he knew Mobile Bay and the Mississippi Sound were already creeping across the island to meet the raging Gulf. Already the water was sweeping objects and probably people in its path like canoes in white water. And the greatest danger was that little drainage ditch next to LeMoyne Avenue. Attempting to cross it and reach Randy's garage at night would be crazy.

I know I promised never to walk on your sacred ground, he said silently. It would serve me right if you killed me dead right now, kill us all in some great ritual sacrifice with the sky full of lightning and thunder booming in our ears till we all went deaf as well as dead. But maybe... maybe you could pity us, especially the others, 'cause they're just following me. And as for me, it was the only thing on earth I could think to do....

As though warned by a voice in his unconscious, or a long submerged memory, Al stopped. "Hold it!" he shouted as others bumped against him. "Stop."

"Stop!" The word went back along the line. He inched forward, kicking his feet beneath the water, until he felt the chain just below his knee. He reached down and lifted it above the surface with the hook where his arm used to be. With the flashlight, he illuminated it.

"Hey, you with the flashlight—Norman," he shouted. "Go down there a ways and lead them over the chain. These are the mounds. Take them on up under the live oaks. It'll stay high and dry there, I believe. Go on folks, follow him now. Step up and over, up and over. Not *through* it, lady—up and *over.*"

———

Some thousands of feet offshore, where torrents of thunderous rain fell on vast swells, darkness reigned. All life retreated. But in the silent depths, 150 feet below the surface, sharks, dolphins, large and small fish, octopuses, squid, shrimp, and other mobile sea creatures gathered in greater than usual numbers. Here they found shelter from the swells that would become great waves, heaving tons of oysters, scallops, crabs, jellyfish, shells, and debris onto the beach, where following waves would bury them beneath a foot of sand.

The greatest swells would not crest as waves along the shore but sweep across the island at depths of 15 or 20 feet, taking with them toothache trees and sea oats, surging into marshes along Mississippi Sound, filling their fresh water with salt, killing newborn shrimp and fish.

The drama on the island held no meaning to the creatures who'd sought safety in the Gulf's depths.

———

Back at the garage, Lou Parrish told Randy in front of Bill, "I guess you could call it a miracle. This guy's wife just called. She's at Abby's place. Sounded okay. She was saying something about lots of water when the line went dead."

CHAPTER XVII

Kneeling on a cushion before the coffee table in her living room, Cookie stared at the flickering flame of the long, white candle, the only source of light in the house. The voice on the portable radio beside her had become an hypnotic dirge: Constance pounding the northern Gulf coast from Destin, Florida, to Slidell, Louisiana, with the eye now fifty miles south-southwest of Dauphin Island and Mobile. A category four hurricane, the surge eight to twelve feet, waves another ten feet above that. Shorelines devastated, blocks of condominiums in Pensacola Beach and Gulf Shores destroyed. Hundreds of tardy evacuees from the West Florida panhandle trapped or missing. Hundreds more believed stranded on Dauphin Island.

Cookie heard nothing. She remembered the typhoons she had survived as a child in Korea, the tsunamis that had wiped out entire villages, her village, her home, long after her father and mother had carried her and her two brothers high into the mountains. Her father had said, "To be safe we must go high, high."

Yet, Randy, who had promised to protect her, had built her house on the ground near the sea at the foot of the dune, and she had never doubted his wisdom. Soon now she would know.

She heard the wind passing overhead, not howling as in her youth, but roaring, as though an endless freight train were passing by.

Earlier, she had gazed out the window toward the dune, and thought it remarkable that even the rain, driven almost horizontal by the wind, passed overhead to fall on the lawn to the north along with branches and debris. Only an occasional flicker of the flame hinted that a feather of air had seeped in from beneath the door or around a window.

She had known that, in marrying Randy and leaving for America, she would probably never see her parents and brothers again. It seemed as though her decision in some way had caused their deaths, and the guilt had haunted her. She had longed for her mother's embracing arms over the years. But she'd been taught from childhood to forsake all in service to her husband. She had dwelt on that, had served Randy with all her heart, body and soul, and eventually it had assuaged the guilt.

Now she had decided to leave him.

Wrapping her arms around herself, she said aloud, "Hold me, Randy. Hold Cookie tight." Slowly, her eyes closed. She rocked back and forth, humming the old Korean lullaby her mother had taught her. Lightning exploded at the windows, thunder crashed. She thought of another time, just a few years earlier, an October morning, when Randy had awakened beside her and said, "Today I'm taking you to paradise."

She'd giggled as he kissed her throat, but he had meant something else. He'd leaped out of bed and slipped into his jeans, pulled a T-shirt over his head and put on his sneakers. "I'll be back in forty-five minutes," he'd said. "Make a jug of iced tea, pack bug spray, a blanket. I'll take care of the rest."

"What should I wear?"

"Anything. Nothing, if you want. You won't have it on long, anyway."

When he returned, he was trailering the *Island Maiden*. It held a blue and white plastic cooler.

"Don't look in there," he told her. He took the large kettle and lid from under the sink, and filled a five-gallon container with water.

"What we doing?" Cookie asked, giggling.

"I told you," he answered, smiling. "We're going to paradise."

He launched the boat at Heron Bayou just before noon and headed at a leisurely speed west through the Sound. It was the kind of day that comes to south Alabama only in October—clear, dry, the temperature in the high seventies. On the far west end of the island the beach was as white as chalk, the water gleaming, reminding Cookie of the moon.

After twenty minutes through the cut, they reached the shore of uninhabited Petit Bois Island. Randy killed the engine and drifted silently into a small lagoon on the leeward side. Near the shore, he dropped anchor. There, in the boat, he shed his clothes, stepped over the side into the waist-high water, threw the blanket over his shoulder, and took Cookie in his arms. He carried her to the shore, opened the blanket and spread it on the sand. Then, slowly, he undressed her.

Gently, while she stood before him, he caressed her neck, fondled her ear lobes, bent to kiss her breasts. He took her in his arms and lowered her to the blanket.

"Be right back," he said. In a moment he returned from the boat carrying the cooler and kettle. Like an adolescent on a campout, he hurried around gathering wood and tinder. With larger branches he made a teepee to support the kettle over the flames. He poured water into the kettle, and ignited the fire. While the water warmed, he took a bottle of champagne and two glasses from the cooler.

"To you," he toasted, touching his glass to hers.

They dined that afternoon on boiled shrimp and corn on the cob. Afterward, he kissed her abdomen and traced with his tongue a line from her navel to her inner thighs and the backs of her knees. She closed her eyes and basked under the warm sun, a light breeze moving across her body, while Randy nibbled her ear lobes and caressed her breasts.

"I love you, Cookie."

It seemed an hour or more before he settled over her, the muscles of his face tense with desire, his eyes narrow, holding hers. She ran her hands over his damp back and buttocks. Higher and higher they grew, moving in rhythm as though rolling on the gentle, undulating waves of the sea.

She heard Randy's moans and whimpers, saw his face distorted with pleasure so intense it looked like pain. She dropped her head back, arching toward him, gasping. Finally, she sighed, and brushed away his tears.

They'd made love twice more that day, and stayed in each other's arms until the final blood-red sliver of sun dropped into the western Gulf.

The phone's ringing startled her. She leaned over to the end table beside the sofa and lifted the receiver.

"Hello?"

"Hi, honey,"

"Randy?"

"I was surprised I could still get through. Is the power out over there?" Although there was crackling on the line, she could hear him clearly.

"Yes. Half hour ago, everything go dark. But I have candles."

"Good. I know you'll be safe. I wanted to call earlier—things're nuts around here. I can't believe it."

"I believe."

"I just want you to know something, Cookie. I..." For a second, static drowned out his words. "...as much as I know how to love anybody. In fact, maybe I love you more than I know how."

"I love you, too, Randy. But you know that."

"Yes, I do. I was thinking just a minute ago about that time we went out to Petit Bois. Remember that—the champagne and shrimp and—well, everything?"

"I remember, Randy. I remember all."

For a moment they were silent. Then Randy said, "Cookie, maybe...maybe we can try again, when this is over."

She said nothing. Then she whispered, "Yes, Randy. Maybe."

"Well," he said, the relief obvious in his voice, "I have to go. I'll be by as soon as I can. Goodbye, Cookie."

"Goodbye, Randy."

———

Two things unsettled Al. One was that he'd lost the CB radio. He'd shoved it in his back pocket, and somewhere along the way it had worked itself loose and fallen out. There was no way to call for help.

The second was that the first didn't matter. No one could reach him. Between the shell mounds and LeMoyne to their west ran that drainage ditch. It began as run-off from Silver Lake in the Bird Sanctuary, little more than a foot-wide trickle to the northeast, running beneath Bienville Boulevard, then paralleling LeMoyne to empty into Little Dauphin Island Bay east of the bridge. But in storm surges, the water moved backward, a wall of it four or five feet high, overwhelming the small ditch and the low-lying land around it, racing over the roads, through the woods, the lake, with force enough to sweep any man off his feet and dump him into the Gulf.

Upon reaching the base of the mounds, he had almost turned west anyway. He imagined the hurricane growing more intense with the morning—in fact, he expected it would. His fifty castaways would futilely attempt to cling to trees and vines, their fingers bloody with the effort. Yet, winds of one hundred fifty miles an hour would hurl them off, dashing their brains against the trees. Others would drown in seething water already eight feet above its banks.

But suddenly absolute peace settled upon him. In his mind, he envisioned the shell mounds. They were illuminated, as though in a blaze of sustained lightning. He saw a forest of live oaks, their trunks four, six, eight feet in diameter, their branches sprawling forty feet, arching down to the ground, each tall on the crest of its own mound. There seemed to be no living beings on the sacred land.

Then, in a crevice between two mounds, some ten feet deep, sheltered by those thick, draping branches dressed in Spanish moss and vines, Al imagined the form of a child, a boy, and beside him a girl. He saw others, men and women, lying flat at the bottom of those gorges, all red skinned and naked or in loin cloths, huddling together, chanting, and these were the spirits of the dead.

"Get them all to the top, but down in the gullies!" Al ordered.

"What about the lightning?" Someone yelled.

"The Sea Lab beacon tower over there is twice as high, and wired for a hit," Al shouted back.

"The trees could be uprooted."

"These trees have been here three hundred years, man—look at them! They been through *twenty* hurricanes. Why? They stand *together*, that's why! They break up the wind like they're one single tree!"

With that, Al started toward the back of the line, tripping over branches and boulders, hurling himself up and on, shouting to the stragglers, bullying, threatening.

Reaching the mounds, the line broke up. Survivors found their own paths in the illumination of the combined flashlights.

After the last straggler stepped over the chain, Norman took Jessica's hand firmly, keeping her behind him. He confronted the sturdy branch of a live oak with his upper lip and nose, staggered back, licked away some blood.

"What happened?" Jessica shouted over the wind. "Are you all right?"

"A mere trifle, Jessica," he answered. He put his hand on Jessica's head and guided her beneath the branch.

Like phosphorescent insects, the flashlights swarmed toward the highest mounds, then vanished in the depressions. But Norman led Jessica along to the eastern side of the rise and finally north, where the muffled glow of the Sea Lab beacon, powered by a generator, illuminated the bulkhead. There, waves thundered against pilings, leaping high over the wall and crashing onto the asphalt parking lot.

Twenty feet above the sea, Jessica and Norman huddled behind the crest of a mound, deafened by the now constant wind. The silhouettes of large objects flew by—a screen door, a twisted hunk of metal. The sea itself joined the madness, tossing a small boat into the bulkhead, splintering it. The wind caught the shattered boards in mid-flight, hurling them into the Sea Lab through glass doors.

Jessica shuddered.

Norman took her face in his hands and turned her ear to him. "It will be all right," he yelled. Jessica searched the impenetrable sky, surveyed the raging sea. Finally, in the beam of his flashlight, he saw the tension in her face relax.

"Try to sleep," Norman shouted. He brought her head to his chest, put his arm around her.

She listened to his heartbeat and felt his lungs expand and contract. Somehow, miraculously, she thought, in spite of the chaos all around them, within a few minutes Norman fell asleep. She herself would not sleep. That was a difference between Norman and her. He accepted life as it came, changing what he could and enduring the rest. Only now was she learning to—how did Norman put it?—float on the crest of the waves.

Of course hurricanes don't play fair. A tornado comes at you quick, gives you its best shot, then vanishes. Constance had begun as a light shower six or eight hours ago. Eventually the rain had fallen more steadily, then a light gust or two. Eventually lightening and thunder, the wind kicking up to a steady blow of 30, 40 miles an hour, the gusts getting serious. Hour upon hour the storm's energy had increased, driving leaves and pine needles and later small branches of trees skimming across asphalt. Hour after hour the din had increased. Loblolly pines snapped off halfway up and crashed into outstretched branches of other trees.

And still it continued building, wearing you down, wearing you down.

It was the intractable, the persistent ever-increasing intensity through half the day and now well into the night with no abatement. It demanded a patience and endurance she might not possess. Yet, she had no alternative.

What had Norman said the other night on the beach? She was really drunk then, no two ways about it. But she remembered: "Every minute every one of us lives on the edge." It's true, she realized. At least the hurricane is honest about it—you see it, hear it, taste its salt in the rain, feel the sting of wind-driven sand, the unimaginable force of it. Not like some shadow on an x-ray.

A deafening crack of lightening and explosion of thunder overwhelmed the wind's howling. Jessica smiled, awed by the display of unfathomable power. Hurry, Norman—save the virgins. She smiled because of Norman, too, sleeping like a baby beside her. But she smiled for another reason as well: She had become resolute: She would be patient and endure.

Throughout the night the storm's intensity grew. Many survivors lay sleepless hour after hour as the water levels grew in the gullies where they nestled before flowing off the mounds and toward the drainage ditch. In the distance they continued to hear trees snapping or crashing, uprooted. Yet, the old trees of the shell mounds stood firm.

CHAPTER XVIII

While Abby Marwick sat next to her best friend with her lips firmly pressed together, Betsy Smith prayed, "If it be Your will, dear God, let us live. And please melt Abby's heart. Please give her faith, and peace, peace—"

Another gust drove into the great room and tore paintings from the wall.

This just isn't acceptable, Betsy said to herself. On hands and knees she crawled across the floor toward the patio door. "Where's the crank?" she bellowed.

"Why? The glass is out!"

"We can still lower the shutters and keep the wind from ripping the roof off!"

"In that table in the corner!"

Abby felt her way along the corridor to the library. It's here somewhere, she thought, lightly brushing her hands across the books. Wish I was just a little bit sober. It's on the middle shelf—just don't know *which* middle shelf, which book case. Why I have all these books in the first place when I don't read…

Her fingers brushed the glass chimney of a hurricane lamp. She felt around its base, found the box of wooden matches. Carefully in the complete darkness she removed the chimney and placed it farther back on the shelf. She felt the wick. It was wet with oil.

Shielding the wick from the wind whipping through the room, she took a match from the box and scraped it against the striker. When it flared, she touched it to the wick and quickly put the chimney on the lamp.

"Hallelujah!" she shouted, then, dryly, "or something."

In the flickering glow of Abby's lamp, Betsy found the table and crank easily. A moment later, just as a window in the rear of the house shattered, the shutter began lowering.

Suddenly the room grew comparatively silent. Betsy started across the floor toward a large window.

"My God, you're bleeding!" Abby shrieked. Betsy looked down at her hands and knees. Blood dripped from small cuts on her knees and palms.

"I'll get some cloths and bandages," Abby said, rushing from the room.

She returned with a bottle of hydrogen peroxide, a pair of scissors, and a new white cotton dress which she cut into wide bandages.

"What'er you doing?" Betsy asked.
"We gotta stop the bleeding"
"It's not a big deal, hardly worth ruining an expensive dress."

"Just be quiet and don't talk. It's my dress." After cleansing the wounds, Abby wrapped them snugly. "Betsy," she said shaking her head, "I hate to see you suffering because of me."

"Don't be silly, I'm not suffering. At least not as much as you did when I climbed the tree and couldn't get down. Remember? You told me to jump—you'd catch me. I can see it now—I practically *buried* you. You sprained both ankles and a wrist."

Abby chuckled and Betsy laughed. Soon they were both laughing uproariously.

"How...did I ever think I could catch you?"

"I supposed you *didn't* think. You wanted to help because you loved me."

187

The two spent much of the night talking. As the hours passed, Abby grew sober.

"You like being a mother?" she asked.

"Oh, yes—more than being a wife, that's for sure. I believe it's the reason I was put on earth."

"Put here, huh?" Abby grew somber. "I don't think we were put here at all. I think we just showed up, and after ten minutes we got so bored we invented wars and religion and perverted sex just to keep from going mad. Sometimes I think the cure may be worse than the disease."

"You're never going to be happy unless you give your life to God, Abby," Betsy said softly. "I think you know that."

For a moment neither spoke. The wind, rushing around and over the dome-shaped house, whined like a child in the dark. Abby took a deep breath and exhaled.

Finally she said, as though to herself, "They're all phonies, every one of them. You're the one exception, Betsy—the one true believer."

Eventually, their thinking muddled by sleeplessness, they carried cushions into the bathroom because it was sheltered from the ocean and small and seemed secure. Betsy slept immediately, but Abby lay awake like a death row inmate awaiting her execution. She had realized when the chair burst through the glass door that arrogance and inebriation had overridden common sense. She had railed at nature, challenged and dared it, and nature had taken it personally.

The Gulf-facing deck and steps had already collapsed. The debris floated below the bathroom window, smashing into the building with every wave. It was only a matter of time before the end. She hoped it would be over quickly, a broken neck or blow to the head. A prolonged death, water filling her lungs, struggling, gasping, finally drowning terrified her. She thought it curious that the inevitable should fill her with such fear. She had never lived as though life held much value. In fact it hadn't. She'd spent it lavishly, tossing her body and her days to the wind as though they were of no worth. At least she might have done something useful, some little thing....

———

Al Reed lay with his face in a puddle, the wind howling above him, tree limbs thrashing the air. The mounds were now shrouded in absolute darkness as one by one the flashlights were extinguished or their batteries died. He could hear the angry waves crashing high over the bulkheads, see flashes of lightning sear the sky. Yet, deep in the gully, surrounded by who knows how many others, Al felt serene, almost blissful. In spite of the raincoat, he was soaked to the skin—they all were, no doubt. It was like sleeping in a tub of lukewarm water. That wasn't so bad. Nor was the thunder—he ignored it. Al was at peace. He thanked the spirits of the dead, thanked them from his heart, humbly and sincerely. Resting his head on his arm, he slept.

———

With morning came a lesser darkness, forms defined in bleak shades of gray, the sky dreadful in its anger. Ruth had been lying next to Don, listening to the weather radio through earphones. Suddenly she struggled to her feet and hurried to Randy's office. She shook Randy's arm, awakening him where he dozed at the desk.

"It just came over the weather radio," she said, her face ashen. "We're getting the whole damn thing. We'll be in the eye in an hour. Just before then and right after, they're calling for one-hundred-fifty-mile-an-hour winds and surges twenty feet above normal. It just might wipe this whole island off the map!"

Bill Smith walked up to Randy, his face twisted in a ghastly wreckage of tears. He opened his mouth to speak, shook his head and dropped his chin to his chest. Randy stood and grasped his shoulders.

"Look, Bill, we're going for them. Look at me." He took the man's chin in his hand and lifted it. "There's this one window. It's the eye of the storm. It won't last long, twenty minutes, half an hour. But if we can get down there in the *Maiden* and be ready when it all gets calm, maybe we can get in there and get them out."

Doyle had been dozing on some cushions in the corner of the office. He heard Randy's words.

"You musta been sniffing glue or doing pot or something, Randy," he said. "You wouldn't get twenty feet off shore with that little puddle jumper before you'd be submerged or capsized, and you know it."

Randy shrugged. "We gotta do something."

"Please," Bill pleaded. "My wife's out there!"

Doyle saw the glassy brightness of Randy's eyes. He wondered for a moment whether it was lack of sleep, or if Randy was actually high.

"We'll take the tug," Doyle said. "It's built for weather."

Randy smiled. "Now there's an idea!" he exclaimed.

"I'll go too," Lou Parrish said.

190

"Yeah, I'm coming along with you guys," said Don Long, who had followed Ruth to the office. She glowered at him.

"Sorry guys," Randy said. "This is a two-man operation. Anyone else is gonna just get in the way." He turned to Doyle. "Let's go Buddy, get this show on the road."

Randy put his shoulder to the door and forced it open against the wind.

———

Abby Marwick stood trembling at the small reinforced bathroom window, one of the few intentionally lacking steel shutters, and stared in disbelief at the fifteen-foot waves crashing over the ruins of the house she'd rented to Betsy Smith. All that remained of it were the pilings. The walls, roof, and furnishings floated on the waves, to be sucked out into the Gulf by the undertow and hurled inland again and again.

Beyond the Smith wreckage, house after house had vanished. All around her, as far as she could see, were destruction, debris, and water.

The storm surge had long since risen to the pilings supporting Abby's reinforced concrete house. With every rush of water back to the sea, the undertow had scraped away at the beach, and now the base of the pilings lay exposed. The one supporting the northeast corner of the house, enduring the most direct onslaught, shifted imperceptibly as the waves burst upon it. Finally, under a barrage of violent attacks, it shuddered, strips of concrete breaking away. The steel reinforcements bent, and a corner of the house fell into the seething froth.

The tile behind the tub vanished, and Abby, staring across the submerged island to the Mississippi Sound, screamed.

CHAPTER XIX

On hands and knees Randy and Doyle made their way along the road to the slip where *Barbara* leaped and plunged like a bug on a hot griddle.

"When we cut the ropes," Randy shouted, "those waves could smash her into the bulkhead!"

"I'll give her full throttle in reverse," Doyle yelled. "If we can get away from the pilings, I think we'll be okay!" He hurried along the finger pier to the stern of the boat, and, studying the water, perfectly timed his leap onto the deck. He pulled out the choke and hastened below to crank the engine. In a moment, it growled into action, and, with the generator charging the batteries, Doyle turned on the bilge pumps.

He allowed the engine to warm up for several minutes before stumbling back to the cockpit and tying additional fenders over the sides. He motioned for Randy to come aboard.

"This is like riding a bucking bull!" Randy laughed.

"Go below and up through the hatch," Doyle yelled. "You got a knife?" Randy nodded. "Just cut the lines right art the cleats—but wait till I wave." Randy moved forward and Doyle made his way to the pilothouse. Depressing the clutch, he threw the gear shift into reverse and opened the throttle. Slowly he released the clutch. The lines tightened as the engine strained against them.

Dashing to the stern, Doyle untied the ropes from the cleats. Back at the wheel, he signaled Randy, who instantly slashed the lines holding the tug to the pier. Suddenly the boat shot backward, the fenders bashing into piles.

Doyle spun the wheel and the boat raced stern-first through the crests of waves and plunged into a trough. Rolling left and right, diving and leaping, *Barbara* finally moved into the channel and headed west.

Even in these waters, sheltered by the island, four-and-five-foot chasing waves surged over the rear port quarter. The boat rose on vast swells and dipped, its bow plunging under the waves to rise again like a submerged cork. Although the windshield wipers were at full speed, the waves breaking over the boat made forward vision impossible. Doyle steered blindly, relying on the dark shadow of coastline and his memory to guide him.

Beside him, Randy stood with legs apart, both hands on safety bars, his eyes wide, smiling broadly.

"You know," Randy shouted, grinning, "Last night, this morning, here, now—it's like all coming together for me. It sounds crazy—I feel really *alive* right now."

Randy stepped out onto the stern deck. One strong, callused hand grasped the rail. The other clung to a handle bolted to the pilothouse wall. Shifting his weight by bending his knees, he rode the pitching, sliding tug flawlessly. The rain beating against his leathery face, he thought of Abby's caress—poor, crazy Abby. He imagined Cookie's sweet smile, and for a moment felt overwhelmed by the wonder of his life.

They had been pounding west for twenty minutes when all at once the wind and rain ceased. The sky directly overhead grew blue and cloudless. The roar gave way to profound silence, and both men heard the tug's swish through the water.

"The eye," Randy said as though to himself.

———

The silence startled Al Reed to full alertness. He sat up, rubbed his eyes and looked skyward to find sunlight filtering through tree branches. All around him lay people, drenched and silent. They were awake, gazing at him with blank expressions. Al leaped to his feet.

"Come on, everybody up!" he shouted. "We gotta get to the garage now, before we get hit by that eye wall again." He saw Norman and Jessica coming up from the depression where they'd spent the night. "Norman," Al yelled, "make sure we don't leave nobody behind."

"I'll do that, Al."

"Norman—you look like hell."

"So I've been told, Al."

Quickly the pack moved like wartime refugees across the mounds to the road that would take them west to LeMoyne and north to DeSoto and the garage. The water was almost knee-deep, spread like a broad river across much of the island, but, with the ceasing of rain, it moved slowly. Only the submerged obstacles posed danger, and Al moved cautiously to find an unimpeded route.

Problem's gonna be the ditch, he thought. Water'll be running like hell through there. I don't know what we're gonna do. No, I don't.

A block from the ditch, he discovered what he took to be another miracle. Maybe the Indian spirits were still looking out for him and his pathetic band. Or maybe Constance herself had shown compassion, although hurricanes weren't supposed to have compassion in their natures. Whatever the reason, there straddling the ditch and crushed like a giant pancake was the roof of Zechariah Ledbetter's general store. It was a monster of a thing, with asphalt shingles lying everywhere, along with shelves, food, and hardware.

"Come on!" Al yelled, his voice growing hoarse. "We're gonna make it. We're saved!"

Some on hands on knees, some upright, the procession stumbled across the roof and into the flooded street. Looking to the left, Al saw that Zach Ledbetter's store had been completely demolished. He and his wife huddled beside the freezer.

"What are you sitting there for, you old fool?" Al screeched. "Get your butt over to the garage before the wall hits again!" Suddenly Zach rose and helped his wife to her feet. They shuffled to join the survivors.

Approaching the marina, some paused to gaze at the smashed hulls of boats strewn across the road. Nearer the water, boats sat on each other like crushed car bodies at a salvage yard.

Norman squeezed Jessica's arm.

"Oh, no," he said softly. My boat—it's gone."

"Stop gawking—keep moving!" Al ordered.

────────

"That's it there," Doyle said, pointing from the tug's pilothouse to the dagger-like shards of 2x4's that had once supported the roof of a pavilion. The pier that reached from it to the submerged shoreline was still intact. A hundred yards beyond it, across the swamped Bienville Boulevard on the Gulf side, the remains of Abby Marwick's concrete house rose above the waves.

"Try to get in closer to the shore, and by the pier," Randy said. "With the storm surge, we'll probably get ten feet from the old shoreline. Look, ain't that Abby waving from—that whole side of the house is gone!"

"It sure is!"

"Get me in close, but *don't ground*. Soon as you feel the bottom, back off before a swell throws you aground. No, forget it. This is close enough. No sense taking chances."

Tightening his own life jacket, with two others tied around his waist and a rope slung over his shoulder, Randy stepped off the gunwale. He sank, popped to the surface instantly and struggled toward the shore, finally touching ground.

"Hey, Randy," Doyle yelled after him, "better get back in fifteen minutes—twenty at the most. These eyes can go by pretty quick."

The world Randy moved through was like nothing he'd known before. The stillness, the warmth of the waist-high water, the tranquility—all seemed unreal. Although he struggled to move through the water, he seemed to be making no progress. It didn't matter.

He was halfway to Abby. Betsy now stood at her side. They waved. Randy lifted his hand, a mechanical gesture from which he felt distanced. He saw the sand had been washed almost completely from around the reinforced concrete pilings, and knew the house could not stand much longer. Yet, he was untroubled. It seemed a violin was playing some long-ago love song.

As he approached, he heard a voice:

"Randy, thank you! Thank you!" Abby shouted. "How're we getting down?"

Perhaps it was the lack of sleep for so many nights. Like a robot, he unhitched the life jackets and tossed them up to the two women.

The music filled his head.

He uncoiled the rope he'd carried over his shoulder, made a knot in one end and, on the first try, hurled it over Abby's shoulder. She and Betsy grasped it.

"Okay, now tie it around your waist, either of you."

Abby held the rope out to Betsy.

"No, you go first," Betsy said. "If I die I'll go to heaven. God knows where you'll end up."

"You've got kids."

"Just *go*!"

Abby obeyed, tightening the rope around her waist.

"Okay," Randy yelled, "jump straight out at me. You'll pop to the surface soon enough I'll pull you to me."

"Well," Abby said, taking a deep breath. "Here goes nothing." She stepped back, ran forward, and leaped.

Gripping the rope firmly, leaning back and digging his heels into the sand, Randy pulled, keeping Abby's head above water. Finally she stood in the waist-high sea and moved to Randy. She gave him the rope.

"Randy," she said, taking his face in her hands. In her eyes, he saw something new, something honest. "I finally know what I want— what I need. I love you, Randy."

"Later," he said, kissing her forehead. "You better get moving. No telling how long we have."

Abby held him with her eyes. She put a finger to her lips, touched his cheek, and started toward the tug. He watched her for a moment, as though she were in a film, moving through silver-blue water, the perfect shape of her, long hair reaching down her back to seductively swaying hips, still in her bra and panties.

He moved back toward the house. "Ready?" he yelled.

"You bet!"

Randy swung the rope over his head twice and let it fly. It was a foot short. Betsy reached for it, lost her balance, and plunged from the bathroom floor. She sank, bobbed to the surface.
With strong strokes she swam to Randy's side.

"God...is teaching me...a lesson," she gasped. "Next time, *I'll*...go first."

Randy laughed and lifted her into his arms. He looked into her pretty eyes, saw her breasts heave. The music in his head soared.

As he stumbled through the water, he imagined it was Cookie in his arms, his beloved Cookie, sweet, always accommodating. She was naked, looking up at him with eyes full of surrender, clinging to him. He gazed down at Betsy Smith and smiled.

Finally, he set her down beside him and led her by the hand. As they approached the pier, he moved more cautiously, searching for submerged debris, mentally drawing a straight line from where he stood to the splintered boards that were once the two-by-fours of the pavilion studding. Finally, he lifted her to the part of the pier where the tug was tied and climbed up himself.

Just as they reached the vessel, the sky grew dark again. Randy lifted Betsy into Doyle's arms and turned to face the sky.

The love song seemed to spread from him across all the still water, rising like vapor on the air. The strains merged with the roar of the wind, a rising crescendo. He embraced the fury with flared nostrils, his eyes bright, arms flung wide, lips parted in a smile.

The wind's impact was instant and furious. It threw Doyle hard to the deck. The women, who had entered the pilothouse, fell against the bulkhead as the tug's bow swung sharply toward the sound.

Laughing into the wind, Randy felt himself rising upward and back, soaring in space. The lightness of his body, the beauty of the storm's fury filled him with transcending joy. It seemed he might never come down.

He fell, plunging into the splintered timber of the pavilion, a spear-like two-by-four piercing his back, protruding from his muscular abdomen, the spike-ravaged flesh skipping lightly over crests of savage waves, arms still outstretched, eyes wide in wonder.

The women's screams rose on the howling wind.

———

Doyle knew that, although *Barbara's* round hull made her more seaworthy in rough weather than boats with hard chines, a rough side-on sea could still capsize her. He worked furiously to keep the bow to the waves, spun the wheel to port, starboard, back to port. For half an hour, he abandoned any hope of making progress to the east. The gale tossed his vessel like so much driftwood—now facing north, now west. He needed to focus every cell of his brain on simple survival as following waves broke over the stern. Yet, he could not rid himself of the unflagging vision of Randy's lifeless body, pierced and spread-eagled, soaring on the crests, vanishing in the troughs, carried farther and farther out to sea.

The *Barbara* heaved, shuddered, plunged. Doyle expected any second she would splinter to bits. He clung to the wheel as much to maintain balance as to steer, while below Betsy and Abby wedged themselves into the tiny head to keep from being tossed about.

Two hours later, Lou and Don, still stood sentinel at the office window. During a few seconds' break in the driving rain, Lou spotted a dark object far out on the water. He lifted the binoculars.

"What's up?" Don asked.

Lou handed him the glasses. "Not sure. I thought—the damn window's streaked, the rain's too heavy. Something's out there. Who knows what?"

"Way out. Yeah. Yeah! I bet you a buck it's them!"

Quickly the men slipped on their rain gear and ran out into the storm. They heaved themselves up the barrier, which had grown by the width of several boats, two cars, and the roof of the Pelican Pub, clamored down, and ran, leaning into the wind, the half block to the docks.

As the tug drew closer, Don and Lou ran out to the end of *Barbara's* slip. The tug's bow crashed down in the slip, bounced off the port fenders, heaved to starboard.

Don studied the waves intently. Suddenly he leaped onto the tug's forward deck, landing flat on his chest and thighs, arms and legs spread. Doyle nudged the bucking vessel forward until Don could grab the line dangling from the pier's cleat. Quickly he secured it to the vessel.

Al raced to the other bowline and tossed it to Don, who still lay on his stomach. He tied it to the boat. Slithering to the hatch, he dived into the boat head-first, raced up the steps past the women and

Doyle, and, bouncing from wall to wall, raced to the stern.

Al was waiting with a line in his hand

With the boat secure, Doyle led Abby up to the cockpit. She had ceased crying. Her face was streaked, ashen. He helped her over the gunwale. Betsy followed, then Doyle.

"Take care of them, guys," he shouted. "They been through hell."

"You don't look so great yourself," Don bellowed. "Where's Randy?"

"They'll tell ya. I gotta see Cookie." He leaned into the wind and moved quickly through the flooded street toward the water tower and the Gulf.

"You won't make it, you crazy fool!" Don yelled.

———

Cookie Manning hadn't seen another human being in twenty-four hours, hadn't talked to anyone since Randy had called the previous night, just before the phone lines went down. In the light of two hurricane lamps she'd lit when the candle began sputtering, she sat on the sofa all night listening to the portable weather radio. The announcer had described the hurricane's movement and severity, had mentioned ham radio operators from Dauphin Island reported severe flooding, but gave no details. For all she knew, she might be the only living person on this ephemeral strip of sand. And that survival she owed to Randy, who had built her this perfect little house nestled at the foot of the dune.

But, she thought, I would rather be dead with him than safe and alone. I hate to be alone.

She heard a banging at the door. It was faint, and she questioned her senses. It could have been a window rattling, some debris hitting the walls. She hesitated.

Again the sound. She hurried to the door, unlocked it, turned the knob. The wind threw it open. Doyle Donahue stumbled in. Together, they forced the door closed again.

He'd run most of the way from the dock. Where the road flooded he'd swum. When he'd grown too exhausted to do either, he rolled onto his back and let the water, racing toward the Gulf, carry him along. As he approached the water tower, he forced his way to the west, toward the great dune and Cookie's house. Approaching the high ground at the foot of the dune, he used the last of his strength to break free of the water, and crawled the rest of the way. Now he stood leaning against the door, gasping.

"Doyle, look at you!" Cookie exclaimed. "You soaked! What happen?"

Doyle was unable to speak.

"Where Randy? Randy okay?"

He led her to the sofa, sitting beside her. Grasping her hand between both of his, he fixed his eyes on hers. "Cookie," he wheezed, "Randy saved…so many…lives today. So many. Al would say he angered…angered the storm gods…taking back…their sacrifices…."

"No!" Cookie cried. "No!"

"He's gone, Cookie."

"Oh!" Just that word, then silence. Tears, profuse tears, but not a sound. Doyle stood and shed his raincoat and hat, pulled a handkerchief from his pocket and dried his face. He sat beside her again, embracing her, holding her tightly to him. Thus, without moving, without speaking, they spent the final hours of the storm.

SATURDAY

CHAPTER XX

On the far west end of the island, the water receded quickly, seeping into the sand, running in newly eroded gullies to the north, west, and south. The sun that Saturday morning lifted tons of moisture into the upper troposphere where it formed puffy cumulus clouds to be carried by trade winds over Georgia and the Carolinas, finally to condense over Pennsylvania, New Jersey, and New York.

The miraculous happened: Some life survived. A raccoon had climbed to the uppermost branches of a toothache tree. Back on the ground, the animal found death everywhere, and feasted heartily.

Sand, spiders and big clawed crabs, having dug ever deeper as the sand above them eroded, came shyly out of their hiding places to investigate the new surroundings, tentatively approaching fish bodies already decaying in the hot sun. They need not have feared the squawking sea gulls, for they had fled the island before the storm, along with the black-bellied plovers and sandpipers, and would not return for days. The insects, too, had vanished.

Few houses stood along the Gulf shoreline west of LeMoyne Avenue. Later that afternoon, a search and rescue party found Milt Goldberg's body under the collapsed roof of his diner.

A few concrete pilings marked the remains of Abby Marwick's house. Remarkably, the Isle Dauphine Restaurant on the beach survived with little damage.

East of LeMoyne, the condos had suffered severe damage and most of the private houses on the Gulf were gone. Along the sound, the storm surge had ruined many homes, and flood damage was universal. Across all of Dauphin Island, white sand covered the landscape like snow.

Several more sections of the bridge had been blown out, and portions of the Pelican Pub were scattered over much of the old village—when Constance passed to the north the wind had shifted and lifted the building from its foundation. A large section of the rear wall leveled Doyle Donahue's home more than a block away.

Manning's Garage had survived structurally intact. Randy's wall of junk had snared tons of debris that would have crashed through the glass front of the building.

Bill Smith's white Plymouth Reliant was never found.

Rescue teams, coordinated by the Civil Defense, searched through debris for survivors, accompanied by an army of journalists, TV reporters, and cameramen. They found a husband, wife and two young children lashed together in the rubble of a house, a Bible clutched to the woman's breast. They were dead. In the old village, a man drowned when his home filled to the ceiling with water. His wife escaped by diving beneath the surface and swimming through a window.

The death toll on the island reached thirty-four, including Milt Goldberg, an elderly couple who had separated from the group heading for the shell mounds, half a dozen who waited too long to flee by boat to the mainland, twelve vacationers who refused to evacuate when warned, and Randy Manning.

Slowly, those who had holed up in Manning's Garage for some thirty-six hours stumbled into the sunlight. Rubbing their eyes, they surveyed the devastation. Some wandered dazed, unable to confront the reality of their personal losses. Others moved zombie-like through flooded streets and lanes toward the rubble that had been their homes.

───

By that afternoon, help arrived from many quarters. A dozen Mobile County deputies came by helicopter to keep the peace. Later in the day, a contingent of National Guardsmen managed to arrive by ferry, after locals towed the debris from Billy Goat Hole. They brought generators, trucks, and armored vehicles. Civil Defense personnel delivered tents, food and water, and eventually the Army Corps of Engineers announced plans to bring bulldozers, front-end loaders, and trucks.

While workmen from the Alabama Power Company hastened to erect new poles and string new lines, a spokesman said, "It will be months before we get power restored here. It's the same story halfway to Montgomery."

Survivors milled around Manning's Garage for hours because they were homeless or had no way to reach the mainland. That afternoon they saw a large helicopter approach from the north and land near what had been Zach's Ship and Shore. Within minutes, it seemed, the Salvation Army and Red Cross set up field tents. Teams passed out food, beverages, dry clothes.

Other helicopters brought the governor of Alabama, some senators and congressmen, all with reporters and journalists. They found piles of rubble to stand beside, answered a few questions, made thirty-second prepared speeches, waved to the bewildered, and left for the next photo op. near Montgomery.

A few private boats arrived at Billy Goat Hole, ferried dozens of vacationers from the island to Bayou La Batre, where emergency shelters and food lines had been established.

On the island, chain saws buzzed, clearing roads of fallen trees. Front-end loaders scooped from the streets several feet of sand, loading it in trucks so it could be dumped back on the beaches.

———

Watching the apparent confusion from the bow of the tug in its slip, Al Reed told Doyle, "It ain't sank in yet. They won't have electricity for six months, no phones for a year. They'll be boiling water here for weeks, won't have gasoline for months—not that there's any place to go, I guess.

"What about food?" Doyle asked.

"They'll truck it in on barges from Mobile. The government'll set up a supply depot, sell us what we need. No scalpers this time. They passed a law."

The two sheriff's deputies who had stopped at Milt's diner earlier in the week looking for Doyle approached. Doyle recognized the tall one.

"Where've you been, Mr. Donahue?" the tall deputy asked.

Doyle looked up at the man then dropped his gaze. "A lot of places Michael. A lot of places. You know the bird sanctuary?"

"Sure."

"Well, there's a tree back in there. I was by that tree for awhile." Doyle stood. He held out his wrists. "You can take me in now," he said.

"What's this?"

"Don't you need to cuff me?"

"You out of your mind?" the shorter officer said. "We don't have time for that now. You just stick around for the next few days. When we get around to it we'll throw the book at you."

"For what?" Al demanded.

"I told you the other day, when you said you didn't know where he was. Leaving the scene of an accident—"

"He was knocked senseless!" Al exclaimed, throwing up his good arm. "He didn't know his own *name* for at least 48 hours."

"Operating that tug under the influence—"

"I'll swear on a stack of Bibles he was sober as you and me. I oughta know, I was with him."

The deputy stared at Al, who glared back. He turned to Doyle, who studied the ground. Finally, Doyle lifted his gaze to meet the deputy's. Neither spoke.

The tall deputy said, "I heard what you did out there with Randy yesterday morning. Coming back practically through the eye wall. How the hell you kept from capsizing I'll never know. You must have stainless steel balls."

"He knows what he's doing is all," said Al. "Best damned captain anywhere."

The tall deputy put his hand on Doyle's shoulder. "So the barge got away from you and you knocked a bridge down. If your pal here says you were sober, as far as I'm concerned you were sober. It's for sure they're gonna slap you with a negligence charge. Don't see how they can win it—pretty obvious it was an equipment failure. And they're gonna try to pull your license. But I sure don't see how anybody can charge you with a crime—my guess is you'll be back pushin' barges before long. *Under* bridges, not through 'em, I hope."

He turned to his partner. "Let's go."

"Now, wait a minute," the short deputy said. "He left the scene of an accident. That's black and white. And it's a crime!"

"For all we know he went for help. Al, did he go for help?"

"He went for help is what he did! I'll swear to it on a stack of Bibles!"

"Let's go," the tall deputy said.

———

Norman Whitney, with Jessica at his side, stepped out of the garage that morning, looked out over the Sound, and rubbed his eyes. He gazed again in disbelief.

"Jessica," he said, pointing, "what do you see?"

"Where?"

"There, right there." Jessica scanned the expanse of muddy water, following Norman's pointing finger.

"It's a boat." She gasped, "It's *your* boat! How on earth—"

"Doyle!" The two ran to Doyle and Al, who were sitting on the bow of *Barbara.*

"Doyle," Norman said, "that's my boat out there. It must be on a sand bar. How about running us out to it?"

"No problem. Hop in."

———

Don Long and Ruth Knebles, alone in the garage, surveyed a landscape of empty mattresses and cots. Together they twisted tiny wires around bread wrappers. Finally, they sat together on one of the cots.

"That was one hell of a storm," Ruth said vacantly.

Don sighed. "The condo's probably gone, you know."

"Big deal. I'm insured."

They were silent. Through the open doors, the blazing semi-tropical sun filled the garage with brilliance. The evaporating water made the air muggy.

"I guess with Randy gone the island's gonna be without a garage," Don said.

"Not necessarily," Ruth answered. She turned to him. "Somebody could open it again."

"Who'd want to do that? Who'd know how?"

"You."

"Oh, sure."

"Well, couldn't you?"

"Well, I guess. But where would I get the money to fix things up, buy tools, rent the building?"

"No, no, you don't rent anything. You buy. I'll buy it all from Cookie, get you started. Look, I refuse to support a man. I'm the old-fashioned type. If you can't pay the bills, I'm outta here."

Don looked around the garage, at the walls and ceiling and concrete floor. Slowly he smiled.

"I could do it," he said. "I could run it like a business, keep Al on part-time, maybe bring in an apprentice, maybe Doyle Donahue. He knows motors. In and out in forty-eight hours, guaranteed. No lawn mowers, no air conditioners, no—"

"No women on the side," Ruth said with a menacing glare.

Don bent and kissed her. "You're a neat gal, Ruth," he said.

Norman eased the *Alicia B.* up to one of the docks at Billy Goat Hole. Jessica stepped off and tied the bow rope to a cleat. Norman secured the stern, and together they walked toward the ferry.

"Did you get much thinking done?" he asked her.

"Some, not much. But what I did was good."

He stopped and pulled her to him, brushing his fingers through her hair, across her ears and down her neck. "I'm going to miss you, my new friend," he said.

"I hope so." She looked at him through eyes vibrant with feeling. "You've helped me more than you know, Norman. I mean that. Will you be staying the whole summer?"

"Yes, I've got to finish the book before September. Jessica..."

She put her fingers against his lips, silencing him.

"I'm going to miss you, too," she said. "But I want us to part happy, not sad. As a matter of fact I've decided I'll definitely be back next summer during July. I expect to make it a tradition, an anniversary celebration of my new life."

"I'll be waiting," Norman said, smiling.

She kissed him, turned quickly, and hurried to the ferry.

For a long while Norman stood gazing toward where she'd disappeared into the crowd. Finally, he walked to the *Alicia B.*, hardly lifting his eyes from the ground. He untied her, started the engine, and headed north toward the Sound and the island's west end.

"So what're you gonna do now?" Al stood beside Lou Parrish near the ferry.

"Go back to New Orleans, wait for the insurance check to arrive, I guess. Then, who knows?"

"Think you'll ever come back?"

"To the island? Only if I go nuts," Lou said, chuckling. He shrugged. "I'm glad I did it. It's something I had to get out of my system, owning my own bar. I'll always have some memories. But this place is halfway between hell and a mental ward."

"I know what you mean," Al agreed, shaking his head and staring at the ground. "Ain't no movie houses, no casinos, not even a bar no more. Or any people to speak of. Guess that's what appeals to me about the place. It's just about as basic as you can find."

Lou shook his head He extended his hand and Al shook it. A moment later he vanished into the crowd on the ferry.

———

Later, Al leaned against a tree and watched the ferry pull away from the dock. The two kids he'd met at the garage, Joshua Smith and his little sister Sara, waved gleefully to the people on the island. Behind them stood Betsy, one arm around her husband, the other embracing Abby Marwick. The way Doyle told it, if it hadn't been for Betsy, Abby'd probably just jumped overboard into the sound to die with Randy. Now she stood there pale and quiet, numb it looked like, outside herself.

The ferry grew smaller and smaller as it moved east, then north, finally seeming to merge into the choppy gray water of Mobile Bay. Its disappearance left Al feeling hollow in his stomach, the way he always felt when he thought of beginnings and endings and how things changed and yet stayed the same. It was so powerful an ache it left him breathless. Yet, he couldn't express it, this feeling and where it came from. Maybe Norman could write it down, but he, himself, was too dumb. In fact he couldn't even understand it, that largeness, that one eternal something that embraced him, pained him, and left him in awe.

———

An hour before sunset, Norman Whitney anchored the *Alicia B.* in the sound at the west end of the island, stripped, and dove into the water. Reaching the beach, he walked across the moonscape of sand, and, the sun bathing his body in a soft red glow, jogged along the beach.